T0313641

ENTERPRISE

02.07

Exit Strategies

Nicolas King

- Fast track route to maximizing investment returns through MBOs, trade sales and IPOs

- Covers the key areas of exit strategy, from setting objectives, choosing your exit route and aligning the interests of investors and entrepreneurs to completing your exit checklist

- Examples and lessons from some of the world's most successful businesses, including Dixons' Internet spin-off, Freeserve, the successful flotation of Delifrance's Asian franchise operations, and Apple Computer's outrageously successful investment in ARM Holdings. Plus ideas from the smartest thinkers and practitioners, including Josh Lerner, Joss Peeters, Will Schmidt and John Wall

- Includes a glossary of key concepts and a comprehensive resources guide

≫EXPRESS EXEC.COM≪
essential management thinking at your fingertips

Copyright © Capstone Publishing 2002

The right of Nicolas King to be identified as the author of this work has been asserted in accordance with the Copyright, Designs and Patents Act 1988

First published 2002 by
Capstone Publishing (a Wiley company)
8 Newtec Place
Magdalen Road
Oxford OX4 1RE
United Kingdom
http://www.capstoneideas.com

All rights reserved. Except for the quotation of short passages for the purposes of criticism and review, no part of this publication may be reproduced, stored in a retrieval system, or transmitted, in any form or by any means, electronic, mechanical, photocopying, recording or otherwise, without the prior permission of the publisher.

CIP catalogue records for this book are available from the British Library and the US Library of Congress

ISBN 1-84112-373-0

Substantial discounts on bulk quantities of Capstone books are available to corporations, professional associations and other organizations. Please contact Capstone for more details on +44 (0)1865 798 623 or (fax) +44 (0)1865 240 941 or (e-mail) info@wiley-capstone.co.uk

MIX
Paper from
responsible sources
FSC   FSC® C013604

Contents

Introduction to ExpressExec

ExpressExec is 3 million words of the latest management thinking compiled into 10 modules. Each module contains 10 individual titles forming a comprehensive resource of current business practice written by leading practitioners in their field. From brand management to balanced scorecard, ExpressExec enables you to grasp the key concepts behind each subject and implement the theory immediately. Each of the 100 titles is available in print and electronic formats.

Through the ExpressExec.com Website you will discover that you can access the complete resource in a number of ways:

» printed books or e-books;
» e-content – PDF or XML (for licensed syndication) adding value to an intranet or Internet site;
» a corporate e-learning/knowledge management solution providing a cost-effective platform for developing skills and sharing knowledge within an organization;
» bespoke delivery – tailored solutions to solve your need.

Why not visit www.expressexec.com and register for free key management briefings, a monthly newsletter and interactive skills checklists. Share your ideas about ExpressExec and your thoughts about business today.

Please contact elound@wiley-capstone.co.uk for more information.

Introduction to Exit Strategies

» Exit strategy – payback time on your willingness to take a risk and back a business project.
» Pre-nuptial agreements.
» The way that entrepreneurs and their venture backers align their interests.
» High-profile designer exits.
» Successful outcomes make the door under the exit sign revolve faster.

It's a bit like a pre-nuptial agreement in a celebrity marriage. In deals of the size that will get an investment banker out of bed these days, say $300mn to $400mn, it's rare for someone not to insist on an explicit exit agreement. An entrepreneur may not see beyond owning and running a business, but most investors want to see a return within three to five years, if not sooner. They are hardly likely to join you in the journey along the path of enterprise without a clear road map for a pay-off.

Agreeing on the likely timing and method of exiting – trade sale, flotation or buy-out – helps give everyone the same mindset for planning the business' development and monitoring its progress.

After all, putting the money or effort in to a business may give you a buzz. But getting out, realizing a return, is what gives you all those choices: to buy that yacht, spend more time with your money or perhaps go through the whole process again. If the exit is payback time, the exit strategy is what increases the chances of making that payback a large one.

What makes it all possible is liquidity, the existence of a market in the shares, or equity, you want to trade. One person's exit from a growing business enterprise is another's opportunity to invest. When the economy is booming, returns are high, money is plentiful, and everybody is happy. Institutions and individuals see the good returns they have made from their investments and are willing and able to commit further funds. When returns are poor, the mood is less buoyant, money becomes scarce, and exiting can become virtually impossible.

Like celebrity divorces, there are high-profile exits. Whatever the current state of the market, you can bet that there are "designer VCs," innovative venture capitalists, hard at work even now. They are anticipating the next hot trend for IPOs (initial public offerings) and creating companies that are custom made for that exit opportunity – something at least as sexy as the biotechs, e-commerce and high-tech stocks.

But it's more common for those involved in an enterprise to under-estimate the value of preparing for disposal. Some prepare for a sale; some have a sale thrust upon them. The 'do nothing' option doesn't always mean you can't reach a successful outcome (see Pizza Express case study, Chapter 2). But anticipating the options usually makes the process that much more manageable.

Part of the value of working through an exit agreement is due to the way it develops commitment and trust between the entrepreneurial team and their investors. Backing an entrepreneurial enterprise involves making a significant commitment and sticking with it, often in the face of considerable uncertainty. One of our case studies, Dixon's launch of Freeserve, demonstrates this exceptional commitment (see Chapter 7).

You can, of course, overdo the emphasis on exit strategy at the expense of focusing on the fundamentals, like building a sound business. No matter how hot the IPO market, how intensely the money is burning a hole in an investor's pocket, none of it will come your way unless you have something worth selling.

Many of the Internet start-ups of the late 1990s overlooked this straightforward principle. They were all about cashing in on the bull market and the reckless mood of investors. The quality of the business proposition, management team, and market potential were subsidiary issues. At the height of the boom, the period between starting a company and floating it on the stock market came down from the typical three to five years to an astonishing 18 months. Everybody wanted to be on the bandwagon and some got caught up in playing high finance instead of concentrating on the bottom line (see the Critical Path example in Chapter 4).

It's never a bad strategy to focus on those fundamentals – making sure the business is on a profitable growth path. The better the company, the fewer problems the management team and investors have on exit. When stock markets are flat and the window for listings effectively closed, sitting tight is often the smartest strategy of all.

That's why, in a sense, driving towards an IPO is always the best default exit strategy. Even though trade sales outnumber IPOs by a factor of five, the IPO remains the desire of many growing new businesses and many investors. Shaping up the new business for a flotation forces all concerned to attend to the issues that count in arriving at a proper valuation (see Driving to an IPO, Chapter 6).

Of course, the exit route you planned in advance may not be the one that finally takes place. It will depend on the opportunities that open up. In the highest quality, best managed business, it still pays to be opportunistic about how and when to achieve your exit.

Delifrance Asia, another of our cases, illustrates that combination of planning and opportunism that characterizes entrepreneurial management at its best. Such was the strength of the Delifrance brand and confidence in its growth potential, the management team not only got the flotation away successfully, against the adverse IPO sentiment in Singapore at the time, they achieved a high price without an institutional placing (see Chapter 7).

And finally, our case study on Apple Computer's investment in ARM Holdings is a reminder that sometimes the best strategy does not come down from on high, but from the bottom up (see Chapter 7). It's one of the most outrageously profitable corporate ventures ever, the kind of successful outcome that makes the door under that exit sign revolve that bit faster.

What is an Exit Strategy?

- » What is an exit strategy?
- » Where the money comes from.
- » Types of exit route.
- » Example: Pizza Express auction.

WHAT IS AN EXIT STRATEGY?

Don't get carried away by that high-falutin' term, strategy. As Henry Mintzberg, the distinguished management writer has pointed out, no one has ever seen a strategy. Strategies exist only to the extent that they feature in people's beliefs about a project or organization. Their power lies in their ability to align their interests and shape people's daily actions.

There's always a tension between the entrepreneur growing the business and the investors that are backing it – friends, family, business angels, institutions, or venture capitalists. Granted, they are sharing the risks of the enterprise (the management team's stake in a big deal is likely to be smaller in absolute terms than a venture capitalist's, but it still represents a big personal risk). And both want some of the same things – to make a return, to cash in on success without jeopardizing the business' future, for example. But their priorities are different: one is focused on creating value, the other on realizing it.

The exit strategy is the way that entrepreneurs and their venture backers resolve this tension and align their interests. Having an explicit agreement, for example on how long funds are to be invested, provides a basis for setting performance targets. Agreeing on the likely method of disposal – usually a trade sale, flotation or buy-out – helps give everyone the same mindset for planning the business' development and monitoring its progress.

What neither can control is the liquidity of the market at the appointed time, which will determine how easy – or difficult – it is to exit. It's the ease with which investors exit an investment and realize the fruits of their enterprise that determines their readiness to back new opportunities.

WHERE THE MONEY COMES FROM

Growth enterprise takes investment. A new business needs help to bring it into the world and at critical stages in its growth. Lots of help: cash, support, encouragement, and professional skills.

It's hardest to find, of course, just when its needed most, in the earliest stages. If the business is not generating enough cash to be self-funding – to provide the working capital and funds required for its expansion – the entrepreneur has to look for help.

It is true to say that more pure start-up capital comes from friends, family, working partners, and business angels than comes from the venture capital companies. In the US, for example, the total of private investments in entrepreneurial companies in 1999 was around $63bn. This is substantially more than the $46bn invested in start-ups by the professional venture capital industry during the same period, a year in which the US venture capital industry hit a dramatic new high. The proportion of informal capital is even higher outside the US, averaging around 94% of the total funds invested in 1999.

Once a business is established, capital is easier to find. Working relationships can be a useful source: suppliers, re-sellers, joint venture partners, and other companies that might benefit from your business are all potential prospects. Then institutional investors, looking for lower risk investments with promising returns, come into the picture.

For an entrepreneur looking to raise money, the main choice is between equity and debt. Debt has to be repaid, unfortunately; it's a drain on cash flow. Equity does not involve parting with any cash – dividends can be deferred until the cash is flowing more freely – but costs more in the long term, in terms of ownership of shares in the business.

In principle at least, the early equity investor accepts greater risk in exchange for better returns in the future. Successive rounds of funding, required to finance continuing growth, should offer investors progressively diminishing returns. In practice, returns from later rounds often turn out to be a better bet.

Venture capitalists have to exercise caution in the investment of their shareholders' funds and are more likely to leave the early stage investment to the informal market. They trade off the prospect of lower returns against the better chances of survival of the new company, often preferring to delay an investment until a later funding round, when a business has a well-developed product, a strong management team, and a healthy looking order book. This is a vital issue in determining whether there is sufficient risk capital available to finance early-stage and expansion-stage ventures, sometimes called "classic venture capital."

In Europe especially, a substantial proportion of venture capital is used to finance acquisitions and management buy-outs (sometimes known as *leveraged buy-outs*) of more mature companies, a more predictable and safer class of investment. The difference among nations is dramatic. In 1999, for instance, 75% of all UK venture capital was used to finance buy-outs, compared to only 4% in the US and none at all in Israel.

The most experienced venture capitalists are in the US, where the industry first came of age. They provide a greater proportion than other countries of the total risk capital funds invested domestically, and the biggest share of classic venture capital as a percentage of gross domestic product: in 1999 the figure was 0.52% of GNP. The average amount invested per company in the US is more than $13mn, compared to less than $1mn in many other countries.

Obviously many factors can restrict individual investment decisions. Things like pension fund regulations, capital gains tax, and government policies, for example. The biggest influence on investment decisions is the liquidity of risk capital, the flow of money available for investment. And the biggest influence on liquidity is the health of the IPO market.

EXIT ROUTES

The main forms of exit, besides write-off of a failed business, are trade sales; sales to a financial buyer – usually another venture capital company; IPO (initial public offering); and the various forms of management buy-in, buy-out and buy-back. The big choice is between selling to a trade buyer or floating on the stock market (see Fig. 2.1).

Trade sales

The number and value of trade sales exceed IPOs almost every year by a wide margin and over a 20-year period by a factor of five. Selling to a trade buyer often produces the best price for a company. The buyer is often a rival business or customer that actually knows how to manage in the sector. They can extract the maximum synergies and efficiencies between the businesses, although reducing overheads often means job cuts. The top management team may have to give up control of the enterprise that they have so recently helped to create or grow. This is

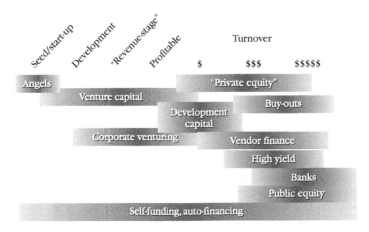

Fig. 2.1 Main forms of exit are trade sales; sales to a financial buyer; IPO (Initial Public Offering); and the various forms of management buy-in, buy-out and buy-back. (Figure from Advent International.)

one of the most common obstacles to a sale and one that the exit plan has to anticipate.

But even when a company is looking for a trade sale rather than a flotation, the prospect of a successful IPO and the valuation of similar companies on the stock exchange influence its market price. Preparing for flotation provides a great shop window for prospective trade buyers.

IPOs

For an existing management team that wants to stay on board, what drives the decision to go public is the need to finance growth and provide scope to pursue new opportunities. Growing businesses are hungry for resources. Internally generated cash flows can't usually keep up with calls on them for new staff, new production facilities, and sales activities in new markets. Shortage of capital is a chronic condition among growing companies.

If successful, an IPO provides an injection of cash for expanding the business – often more cheaply than other sources of finance. The higher profile of a listed company and its visible share price confers some useful advantages, not least the chance to finance acquisitions by issuing shares, giving a faster route to growth.

But it costs a bit, too. As much as 20% of the proceeds of the flotation can disappear to underwriters, bankers, and legal advisers. Then there's the management time and attention on preparation, organization, and seemingly endless roadshows for brokers and fund managers. And with fewer and fewer institutions controlling more and more of the share-buying muscle, it's a case of the bigger, the better. Trading in shares in smaller quoted companies is often too thin to provide the liquidity that was the reason for the flotation in the first place.

That's why, in spite of growing competition from newer stock markets like the AIM (Alternative Investment Market), the London New York Stock Exchange, and NASDAQ, the major markets for new issues in North America are still the primary targets for a listing for ambitious growth business.

Public offerings take a good deal of planning. Internet companies managed to condense the time scales in many cases but, typically, a company has a 3-year track record and has had three or four rounds of funding, private placements by venture capitalists or corporate venturers, by the time it comes to the market. The state of the IPO (initial public offering) market is the main factor in determining the likely return to investors and, hence, the availability of money for new enterprises.

An IPO is not an exit in the same sense as a trade sale, as shareholders and existing management are likely to remain in place following a flotation. Lock-up agreements very often bar insiders from cashing in on the flotation. Venture capital investors may have to keep a significant proportion of their investments – if not the entire stake – for a couple of years to inspire confidence in institutional investors and promote the share price. It is only when they have sold the stock that they have made their exit.

Financial buyers

Venture capital and corporate venture finance provide the successive rounds of funding that new companies require to get in shape to go public and the liquidity that enables early stage investors to exit. Private equity firms are in business to make money for themselves and their investors in a slightly different way.

They buy and extract value from companies that have stalled; or are part of a larger company that no longer wants to be in a particular business; or that have no obvious successor to a chief executive. Once the investor has spent time and money shoring up the business, it will seek to get its money back, plus profits, though an exit.

MBOs/MBIs

Management buy-outs and buy-ins allow entrepreneurial management teams to buy divisions of larger companies as they divest themselves of non-core subsidiaries to focus on their core business. A management buy-back occurs when the management of a new company that no longer needs outside investors to finance its growth takes control of the company by re-acquiring all the shares.

MBOs are often a recipe for unleashing new entrepreneurial skills, improving the results of often underperforming businesses, and creating smaller, more flexible enterprises. They also provide a solution to the family succession issue currently facing a large number of Continental European companies. Post buy-out performance is often characterized by significant increases in turnover.

EXAMPLE: PIZZA EXPRESS
Private auction, the "do nothing" exit strategy

In October 1992, Peter Boizot, founder of the Pizza Express restaurant chain, faced up to the fact that he had no alternative but to sell the business. Like many people in a similar situation, he had never planned for this outcome. Built up over 25 years, Pizza Express had grown steadily to 59 restaurants. Profits, however, had fallen and partner Hugo Carlisle insisted on realizing his stake. Fortunately Boizot's nephew, Mathew Allen, an experienced financial operator, could advise him. With the help of Ernst & Young, the company's auditors, they organized a private auction, which eventually resulted in a highly successful deal. But they could have avoided a lot of grief if they had adopted an exit strategy earlier in the business' life.

Having ruled out a minority shareholder or going public, given recent results, the business' size and the stock market's current state, a buyer seemed the only answer. The pair believed an auction would generate healthy interest in Pizza Express. A sales memorandum sent round by Ernst & Young yielded numerous potential buyers. More than 40 replies arrived, ranging in price from £5mn to £11mn. Via a two-phase auction process, Boizot and Allen formed a shortlist of four: a trade purchase; an MBI/MBO; a venture buy-out and a reverse takeover.

Over a series of meetings with prospective buyers, it became clear Carlisle favored the MBO structure, led by Clive Shell, Pizza Express' finance director, and Roger Hawthorn, the franchise director. But Carlisle's support cut no ice with Boizot, who couldn't imagine Pizza Express being run by a team he had recruited. Boizot and Allen favored the reverse takeover proposed by G + F Holdings, the largest Pizza Express franchisee. While they negotiated with the G + F team, they kept their options open to maintain interest. But the financial pressures were mounting and everyone knew they needed to close soon.

Worried about the impact on business performance if they turned down the MBO bid they promised Shell and Hawthorn a "success fee" of £30,000 even if their bid was rejected, just so long as the company continued operating efficiently.

As Allen's conviction grew that the G + F deal was viable, Boizot was still having difficulties with the reality of having to sell. Finally, Boizot committed to the deal and it only remained to convince the minority shareholders. After heated and near litigious discussions, Carlisle finally agreed to the deal. Following due diligence and some last-minute prevarication, the shareholders agreed to the acquisition, the placing and the rights issue. The Pizza Express offering in February 1993 was a great success; the placing ten times over-subscribed and the share price closed at a 100% premium.

The whole process took about six months. A planned exit might have cut out the lengthy timescales, problems with minority shareholders and the need for a "success fee" paid to the unsuccessful MBO team.

The Evolution of Exit Strategies

- » Leveraged buy-out.
- » Venture capital and corporate venturing.
- » Academic research on harvesting investments – cashing in at exit time.
- » The return of the leveraged buy-out.

It's important to remember that the industry that supports investment in business enterprises is relatively young. Interest in enterprise as a management topic is quite recent and the appreciation of its finer points, like the best way to exit investments, is even younger.

After World War II, the main subject of the rapidly-developing discipline of management studies was the large corporation. Large companies were the main engines of economic growth in America and the English-speaking world, and the main source of demand for management training. Few took much notice of the mid-sized companies that were so important in the rebuilding of Germany's post-war industry.

It was only after the dominance of the Fortune 500 companies started to decline in the 1970s that the management gurus started to cast about for alternative forms of economic success. Recession in the early 1970s, following the oil crisis, and again in the 1980s, heightened interest in whether enterprise and entrepreneurial management could offer a route to growth that avoided the usual pitfalls of the economic cycle.

In the 1980s, shareholders were mainly concerned with performance. They expected company managers to make underperforming assets sweat or, if they couldn't, to sell them. They preferred companies that stuck to what they knew best – and regarded any management team that stepped outside its core business as little short of delinquent. They viewed attempts at diversification with suspicion.

A wave of company bust-ups aimed at refocusing onto core strategy soon followed, starting first in the US when it became clear that the Reagan administration was not going to interfere too much in mergers and acquisitions. One of the most popular ways of pursuing this restructuring was the *leveraged buy-out*.

Leveraged buy-out firms specialize in helping entrepreneurs to finance the purchase of established companies and underperforming divisions of large companies. The approach is to provide a management team with enough equity to make a small downpayment on the purchase of a business, and then to pay the rest of the purchase price with borrowed money. The assets of the company are used as collateral for the loans, and the cashflow of the company is used to pay off the debt.

Because the acquired company is paying for its own acquisition, these investments were originally known as "bootstrap" deals. Eventually they became known as leveraged buy-outs (LBOs), or, in Europe, simply as management buy-outs (MBOs).

Leveraged buy-out firms routinely tried to profit by dismantling the companies they had acquired and then selling off the pieces. The theory was that by breaking up a company, you could alert buyers to the true value of the company's assets, and profit from their sale, one by one. The strategy proved a financial success, but a public relations disaster. By the late 1980s, the business press was regularly attacking leveraged buy-out firms for what they saw as rampant greed.

This was obviously too good to miss and the UK and the rest of Europe soon followed suit. But by the 1980s, corporate raiders like James Goldsmith had gained an unsavory reputation. The peak of notoriety came in 1984, when buy-out firm Kohlberg, Kravis & Roberts financed the $25bn leveraged buy-out of RJR Nabisco, with debt from the junk-bond house Drexel Burnham Lambert, the West Coast office of which was headed by the infamous Michael Milken.

The crowning blow came in 1987, when the movie *Wall Street* cemented in people's minds the image of Gordon Gecko, the callous financial buyer (played by Michael Douglas) taking over companies simply to sell off their assets at the expense of blue-collar jobs. "Greed is good," Gecko told his fictional shareholders.

By the early 1990s, few leveraged buy-out firms were pursuing "buy-and-bust" strategies any more. But the damage to their image had been done. Many decided that the answer was to call themselves something new. They settled on "private equity firms," an innocuous-sounding and more ambiguous name than the phrase it replaced.

For buy-out firms, the attempt to rename their business was only a partial success. The press by and large still refers to them as leveraged buy-out firms, or LBO firms. However, firms did succeed in getting private equity into the lexicon. More commonly, however, people use the term in a broader sense to describe any investment strategy that involves the purchase of equity in a private company, including venture capital and corporate venturing investments.

VENTURE CAPITAL AND CORPORATE VENTURING

During the 1960s and 1970s, venture capital firms focused their investment activity primarily on starting and expanding companies. More
often than not, these companies were exploiting breakthroughs in
electronic, medical, or data processing technology. Early successes
include, for example, Intel Corp., Apple Computer Corp., Lotus Development Corp., Genentech Corp., and Federal Express Corp. As a
result, venture capital came to be almost synonymous with technology
finance.

Venture capital firms tend to specialize by stage of investing. There
are no hard and fast definitions for these stages. Roughly speaking,
however, *seed-stage* firms tend to provide a few hundred thousand
dollars, and perhaps some office space, to an entrepreneur who needs
to flesh out a business plan. *Early-stage* investors back companies at
a point where they have a completed business plan, at least part of a
management team in place, and perhaps a working prototype. Later
stage investors typically provide a second or third round of financing,
often of $10mn or more, that funds production, sales, and marketing,
and carry the company into the revenue-producing stage. *Mezzanine*,
or *pre-IPO-stage*, investors provide a final round of financing that helps
carry the company to an initial public offering.

Companies had started setting up their own corporate venture funds
in the US in the mid 1960s, a couple of decades after the private
venture capital industry. Companies saw the success that the private
venture capital specialists were having with investments, particularly
in technology companies. As so often happens, one deal became a
beacon.

In this case, it was the monumental return that American Research &
Development Corporation made on the start-up financing it provided
in 1958 for computer maker Digital Equipment Corporation. By the
early 1970s, almost one quarter of Fortune 500 firms had tried their
hand at one kind of corporate venturing program or another.

From the 1990s until recently, a series of political and technological
revolutions has relentlessly driven forward public interest in the topic
of enterprise.

The collapse of Communism in the late 1980s unleashed market
forces in Eastern Europe and the former Soviet Union that fed on

a century of underperformance. A rush of Western capital into the economies of Poland, Hungary, Czechoslovakia, and Russia mopped up some of the best investment opportunities to transform privatized business. But the increased liquidity suddenly made raising money much easier and allowed local entrepreneurs to seize on opportunities hitherto denied them.

Even before the Internet, the field of technology fuelled interest in enterprise. Silicon Valley and academic centers like Stanford and MIT became synonymous with new technology. It was no accident that the high-tech sector served as a testbed for entrepreneurial management. High returns, huge investments, a shortage of talent, constant need for education, training, and recruitment of women to the workforce – the technology sector had all the ingredients and provided the earliest indications of constraints to enterprise.

Then, in the 1990s, the Internet changed everything. It attracted the largest slice of speculative investment since the Klondike gold rush a century earlier. Institutional investors and day traders backed e-entrepreneurs indiscriminately. It created an avalanche of opportunities for venture capitalists in the mid and late 1990s.

As a result, the equity capital industry has experienced extraordinary growth in the past few years, both in the number of firms and in the amount of capital they have raised. In 1999, for example, 186 venture firms in the US raised $35.6bn for new investments. That was up from the 161 that raised $19bn the year before. Individual and institutional investors flocked to venture capital funds as returns skyrocketed beyond those available in other asset classes.

Eventually the strong returns that risk capital has offered shareholders in the past decade, in a highly competitive market, have woken up the business schools and management journals. There's an overdue interest in investing in enterprise.

WHERE WE ARE TODAY

There are now centers of excellence in enterprise and entrepreneurial management worldwide: Babson College and the Kauffman Center, for example, in the US; the London Business School; and INSEAD, which, in conjunction with 3i, the venture capital company, has set up a research center in entrepreneurial management in Fontainebleau

(France). INSEAD has a campus in Singapore, from which to compare differences in enterprise culture between Asia Pacific and Western markets.

At last we are starting to collect reliable data on the prevalence of enterprise and understand cultural differences. Perhaps for the first time it is becoming possible to go beyond the stereotypes and draw practical conclusions for companies and policymakers. Among other studies, the Global Entrepreneurship Monitor confirms the relationship between economic growth and enterprise with evidence from a continuous study conducted in 21 countries.

Since the late 1990s, the biggest names in the field, Paul Gompers and Josh Lerner of Harvard Business School, have analyzed the record of venture capital and corporate venturing programs and separated the cyclical factors from the management issues. This has helped put the current activity in context.

However, most of the interest has focused, naturally, in comparing the performance of investments in enterprise against alternative projects. One recent large sample study by Gompers and Lerner, comparing corporate venture investments and venture capital investments, found that when corporations invested in activities that were related to their own line of business, their returns were actually competitive with those of private VC funds.

Academic research on harvesting investments – cashing in at exit time – tends to focus on the sales or IPO process at the time it takes place, rather than on the benefits of planning exits in advance (see Chapter 6, Does exit planning really make a difference?).

Most of the work on exits has come from within the venture capital industry like the Exits Committee of the European Venture Capital Association. This is mainly at the level of observation from practical experience in the market (see Chapter 6, Managing the business for exit).

RECENT MARKET ACTIVITY

Since the Internet crash and the slump in technology stocks have led the downturn on the stock markets, people are sitting tight. Exits have been slow since the start of 2001, down by 42% on 2000's run rate. The proportion accounted for by receiverships has risen to around 44% of recorded exits.

Buy-outs from receivership are on the increase – they more than doubled to provide 11% of the deals to date in 2001.

THE RETURN OF THE LEVERAGED BUY-OUT

The buy-out market often goes against the grain of stock market activity. As companies are pre-occupied with their own problems, the mergers and acquisition market slows to a trickle but there are bargains to be had in non-core, underperforming divisions. This gives existing management teams the chance to step in with an offer, backed up by private equity specialists eager to get in at the bottom and maximize their returns.

Tom Lamb, managing director of Barclays Private Equity says:

> "With most potential trade buyers increasingly distracted by their own trading difficulties the private equity houses are well placed to go bargain hunting, particularly where there is a forced seller. Cash is king."

The situation provides plenty of opportunity for management teams, and their backers, who are the key to the value of a business. In a flat trading environment, they are unlikely to face much competition in the bidding process.

The LBO business has changed dramatically since the buy-and-bust days of the 1980s. The buy-and-bust approach rarely works any more, largely because companies today are so highly priced. In addition, banks and other lenders today are much more conservative about lending money for leveraged buy-outs.

As a result, buy-outs today are financed with more equity. In addition, the companies acquired are usually divisions being sold by corporations that are refocusing on their core businesses, or businesses owned by families who wish to cash out.

To earn an attractive return on their investment, LBO firms today must build value in the companies they acquire. Typically, they do this by improving the acquired company's profitability, growing the acquired company's sales, purchasing related businesses and combining the pieces to make a bigger company, or some combination of those techniques. Consolidation, or "buy-and-build," is now the order of the day, rather than "buy-and-bust."

TIMELINE

» **1958**: American Research & Development Corporation makes monumental return on the start-up financing it provided for computer maker Digital Equipment Corporation; achieves reputed annualized rate of return of 130%.

» **1980s**: More than 100,000 companies now use electronic data interchange.

» **1984**: Kohlberg, Kravis & Roberts finances the $25bn leveraged buy-out of RJR Nabisco, with debt from the junk-bond house Drexel Burnham Lambert (head of West Coast office: the infamous Michael Milken).

» **1985**: Venture Economics starts collecting the data to calculate the return on venture capital investments in the US.

» **1989**: Tim Berners-Lee invents the World Wide Web.

» **1991**: Cisco Systems, the data networking company, launches Cisco Connection Online, a network for vendors, partners, and customers.

» **1994**: Jeff Bezos founds the on-line bookstore, Amazon.com.

» **1995**: Michael Hagen and Michael McNulty found VerticalNet, to operate industry-specific on-line communities.

» **1996**: Cisco adds on-line ordering to CCO, making it one of the first private exchanges.

» **1999**: B2C wobble starts; B2B seen as the real way to make money for investors, as B2B transactions to the value of $85bn take place on-line.

» **2000**: B2B bubble starts to pop in March; high-tech bubble bursts around May; venture capitalists retreat, dotcom marketplaces postpone IPOs; big shake from August onwards.

» **2001**: A succession of dotcom marketplaces fail, merge, or adapt to new business model.

The E-Dimension

» Early stage investment.
» The corporate tail wags the dog.
» Selling up, not out.
» Critical Path, an archetypal dot-com exit.

Many companies are still licking their wounds from a tangle with e-business. Some are more wary than ever about investing, having seen their market valuation, the currency they use to make investments, take a beating. The way that liquidity – the fuel that allows investors to exit their investments – plummeted on the way down from the boom was exceeded only by the speed with which it grew, on the way up.

The e-commerce boom started with some exciting new technologies and lots of bright ideas. Venture capitalists came in and threw money at those ideas. As a business emerged, investment bankers sold stock to an all-too-eager public. With only a limited number of shares available, stocks of these exciting new companies soared. The flood of money that followed led to a funding frenzy.

All that money attracted a new type of Internet entrepreneur. For the first generation of Internet executive, it was a true adventure. The later generation was attracted by the huge market capitalizations and the options. From 1994 to 1998, it was a question of changing the world. By 1999, it was much more about greed.

Still, venture capitalists were able to reap huge returns as investment bankers pushed fledgling businesses through an IPO at an ever-earlier stage in their development. The traditional financing model for a growth company got well and truly squeezed. The time span from formation, through early stage funding, then development, to an IPO, which had been typically three to five years, now collapsed towards 18 months. Internet time, it seemed, applied to realizing a return as well as everything else.

In terms of investment activity, the Internet shifted the focus of funding in the second half of the 1990s dramatically in the direction of early stage investment. Before the Internet boom, a significant proportion of risk capital went into management buy-outs (also called leveraged buy-outs, see Chapter 3), perhaps 25% of the total in North America, but as much as 66% in some parts of Europe. As investors and corporates sought to cash in on the boom, up to 90% of the funding went into the riskier end of the scale.

BRICKS AND CLICKS

Companies embraced e-commerce in different ways. Some, like American Express, leveraged their core business, extending the full range of its services into the e-arena. Spurred by the desire not to miss out on the IPO boom, others were tempted to run Web-based activities at arm's length, with the aim of floating and realizing value – unprecedented value.

In many cases, the corporate tail wagged the dog. The valuation of new economy stocks screamed off the right-hand top corner of the chart, leaving old economy companies in the doldrums. In 1998, the UK electrical retailer Dixons launched Freeserve, an ISP (Internet Service Provider), making the most of its position as one of the largest PC sellers – through its chain of PC World computer stores – to develop an instant customer base. Salespeople signed up buyers to a free proposition without much difficulty. Within 18 months they floated Freeserve on the London Stock Exchange. At the offer price of £1.50 a share Freeserve was valued at a remarkable £1.51bn.

Remarkable indeed, as in just over seven months' trading to May 1 1999, it incurred a net loss of £1.0mn on revenues of less than £3.0mn. The public flotation valued the new company at five times the price of the parent business, a business with more than 50 years of history (see case study in Chapter 7).

Another temptation was for companies to use the inflated value of their Internet interests to acquire "bricks-and-mortar" companies at a discount.

As the new millennium began, greed became pernicious. Investors bought stocks for no other reason than that they were going up, hoping to sell at the top after one more doubling of the share price.

Around March 2000, the virtuous cycle turned vicious. Signs started to crop up that the economy and Internet growth rates were cooling. Second-quarter results at companies like eBay and Amazon proved that revenue growth was slowing dramatically and investors suddenly wanted out. The IPO market dried up. Without hope of taking start-ups public, and with the value of their own funds sinking, VCs stopped funding risky ventures. Eventually, the investment banks wouldn't help raise money for the very same companies they had brought public a year earlier.

With hindsight, the gravity-defying enthusiasm for dotcoms and B2Bs only postponed the downturn in the economic cycle, as business confidence – and consumer spending – fuelled one of the longest sustained periods of growth in economic history.

The fallout from the Internet boom has changed the investment picture dramatically. The initiative has swung back towards the investors, rather than the borrowers. Whatever the outlook for the economy as a whole, it's unlikely they will be so indiscriminate again. Those that wanted to make a quick buck are gone. Those that remain are becoming tougher and tougher.

First they just demanded dotcoms show a path to profitability. Now they also want to see reasonable valuations for Web-based companies, relative to their offline peers. Even Internet companies that pass these more stringent tests are suffering from the Internet hangover: companies used to be pushed out for a flotation too early and now they are being expected to deliver too early.

The amount of money venture-backed companies raised in the US, the world's largest venture capital market, dropped by more than 60% in the 12 months following the Internet boom. Similarly, corporate VC activity was down by more than 80%, the amount available reduced by failed ventures, which reduced corporate earnings.

Many corporations are still dealing with the trauma of seeing their public-market valuations – the currency they use to make investments – take such a beating. Undoubtedly, some have grown wary after watching failed ventures depress their corporate earnings. But the shake-up is also creating opportunities for some traditional companies to build dotcom businesses. With established brand names and with the competition from dotcom start-ups subsiding, they have the deep pockets to build e-commerce that integrates with their traditional lines of business. Take Wal-Mart, which is only now making a serious effort to sell on-line. Or John Lewis, the UK department store and supermarket chain: in the first quarter of 2001, they acquired the UK arm of buy.com for a fraction of its value at the height of the boom and merged its technology sales under its own johnlewis.com brand a year later.

A lot of impatient money went on the Web, betting on e-commerce investors and entrepreneurs who became obsessed about making a quick fortune. When the bull market ran out of steam, some sought an exit at almost any price (see the section on *Critical Path* later in this chapter). Now the e-commerce frenzy has dwindled. But there's still plenty of opportunity to build a valuable brand, create some decent jobs, and even – yes – make some money.

And there are the dotcom survivors, employees who left secure jobs, exposed themselves to a short, sharp course in entrepreneurial management, and lived through the pain of seeing their stock options evaporate. A generation that is now, boomerang fashion, trying to go back where it started or biding its time for another try (see "Selling up, not out").

SELLING UP, NOT OUT

The long-running Internet boom contributed to a new type of exit, one where the owner founder sells up but stays on as part of a larger organization. You may not be the CEO any more, but the best way to make your business grow might be to sell it.

High sale prices meant it was a good time to sell. But it was also a good time to sell out and stay on. A tight labor market meant that many companies wanted to retain both the founding entrepreneur and the company's staff.

While selling out and staying on may strike most entrepreneurs as the worst of both worlds, it can offer a solution to growth for pragmatic owners. For these owners, the sale of their companies is not a get-rich-quick exit strategy but a long-term investment to help take their businesses to the next level. You have to be realistic about deciding how the company will be most successful.

Take expansion. It's expensive, but if you don't grow, you risk losing out to better-financed competitors. An acquiring company may be able to provide the resources, connections, and expertise you lack. The alternatives may not be so attractive, either. Going public may not be an option. Even if you can find one, a venture capital firm's investment isn't problem-free, as it is likely to demand a big stake in your company.

Lisa Hammond sold her promotional-marketing business to a larger Californian e-commerce company, MadeToOrder.com, because she felt her company lacked the technological expertise to go it alone in the Internet economy. MadeToOrder went to great lengths to keep Hammond and her 23 staff happy, even to the extent of accommodating her employees' needs for flexible work schedules. Hammond, now vice-president for merchandising, negotiated both the terms of her own continued employment and the role of her employees. She says:

> "I feel like I'm back doing what I love to do, focusing on the creative spin of the business. As for the people who have been with me – some of them since the beginning seven years ago – I feel I'm giving them opportunities that I couldn't have given them on my own."

Going from CEO to a salary check isn't for everyone. Independent-minded entrepreneurs often find it hard to suddenly take a back seat. Roderick Robertson intended to stay on when he sold Great Eastern Premium Pet Co, his $10mn pet-supply distribution business in Boston, to a group of private investors in 1999. But about two months into the new arrangement, Robertson felt superfluous.

> "All of a sudden, you're on the outside looking in. I went to a meeting once and there were four people in the room. And one turned to me and said: 'OK, Rod, we'll call you if we need you.' I was shocked. I was always the one sitting at the table."

By mutual agreement, Robertson departed. He now runs a small company that makes promotional CD-ROMs. "The flexibility to call my own shots far outstrips the security of a big ship," he says.

How do you know if selling but staying on is the right strategy? First, honestly gauge your commitment to sell and your stomach for ceding control. The emotions of the owner are often a bigger obstacle than price.

In addition, carefully review the non-financial aspects of the deal. Consider how your work cultures will mesh and whether you share a vision for your product and market. How will you manage personnel issues, not just for yourself but for your employees? Will there be changes in the compensation strategy? In benefits? In work processes? Before you sign a deal, nail down all the personnel details, from executive changes to seating arrangements. And don't forget to clarify your own role and title, as well as incentives, stock options, and other compensation.

Ultimately, entrepreneurs who have sold their companies with the intent of staying on offer this advice: Keep sight of what you really want. If it's time to get out, fine. But being acquired could give you the potential to put your knowledge and efforts into something that could truly grow larger that you would have been unable to do by yourself.

CRITICAL PATH, AN ARCHETYPAL DOTCOM EXIT

As recently as January 2001, analysts were issuing "strong buy" ratings and urging clients to buy stock in Critical Path Inc., a promising young company that managed e-mail for corporations.

Its leaders made a critical error: like many other dotcom execs during those manic years, they became slaves to Wall Street instead of focusing on building a long-term business. What emerges is a cautionary tale about a company that put too high a value on prettying itself up for a sale, rather than focusing on its business.

According to interviews with current and former Critical Path executives, once CEO Douglas Hickey and his team had decided to sell the company, maintaining a high stock price trumped all other business fundamentals. Once they set on that course, move after move propelled them down a disastrous road.

On January 18 2001, Critical Path reported a loss of $11.5mn, on revenues of $52mn. This was nowhere near the forecast of $700,000 in profits and $55mn in sales that the company had been giving Wall Street. Within 24 hours, 10 analysts downgraded Critical Path's stock, which tumbled 64%, from $25.13 the day before the announcement to $9 the day after. But the real bombshell came on February 2, when the company disclosed that its fourth-quarter earnings report might have contained accounting irregularities. In a matter of days, 88% of Critical Path's market capitalization and $1.7bn in shareholder value had vaporized. Since then, things have grown worse. In the quarter ended March 31 2001, Critical Path said revenues declined to $27.2mn, and its net loss, excluding special charges, was $42mn. On top of that, at the time of writing the company is facing an investigation by the Securities & Exchange Commission and more than 24 shareholder lawsuits, claiming that the company artificially inflated its stock with unrealistic revenue and profit projections. The stock now trades below $1 per share.

What happened? This high-flyer had seemed so promising. In March 1999, when Critical Path had an initial public offering on Wall Street, the stock immediately soared from $24 to $65. During 2000, it emerged as the leader in its market for handling e-mail for corporations, a $570mn market that is expected to grow to $780mn by 2002, according to market researcher IDC. Critical Path's reported sales were growing 35% a quarter, and its high-profile management team had beefed up its product line with ten acquisitions over two years. Why was it that what had started as a dream of building the Internet future ended up as a cynical exercise in seeking quick profits? According to current and former employees, sales and executive meetings turned into unbearable pressure cookers, as staff members were told to meet their numbers at all costs so that the company could impress analysts and prospective acquirers.

Most of Critical Path's acquisitions were carried out to harvest the revenues and customers of the acquired companies, instead of adding compelling technologies that improved its own core business. That left the company's culture in tatters as it tried to glue together 1000 employees from 10 different companies. "It was just total chaos," recalls Jerry Seikel, a former Critical Path account executive.

Making matters worse, there were possible violations of accounting rules by Critical Path executives who were trying to prop up revenues. According to several current and former executives, the company backdated sales contracts, pushing deals back by several days to count in an earlier quarter. It also relied on so-called side-letter deals, which made it appear as if Critical Path's services were being ordered up by clients when instead they knew this would allow customers to renege on purchase agreements without penalty. "The line between right and wrong wasn't just blurred. It was wiped out," says a former sales manager.

Critical Path officials concede there were accounting irregularities but contend that they were spearheaded by a few individuals who are no longer with the company. Since uncovering the problems, the board has pushed out Hickey, president David Thatcher, and sales vice-president William Rinehart. The company revised its third- and fourth-quarter sales figures for 2000 downward by a total of $19.3mn, nearly one-fifth of the sales it had originally claimed.

Founder and chairman David C. Hayden, who stepped in as interim CEO in February 2001, says he was not aware of the problems when they occurred and that they will not recur.

"The financial events that impacted the company earlier in the year are behind us and were clearly isolated incidents . . . We have put the necessary controls in place both in terms of systems and personnel to ensure that those events will not be repeated in the future." Now Critical Path is fighting for its life. Hayden has streamlined the company's offerings from 40 products and services to a dozen. He has cut the workforce by 40% to 650 employees. And he is attempting to preserve its $171mn in cash. But even Hayden knows a comeback will be difficult. "The start-over effort will be more challenging than the start-up phase," he says.

Critical Path was steeped in idealism at its birth. In 1997, Hayden and a group of programmers set out to build a world-transforming business, creating an e-mail service that they hoped would be used by thousands of corporations and millions of employees. Their goal: to turn e-mail into a simple utility, much like water or electricity. Critical Path would run all the software and deliver e-mail accounts to corporations, which would pay them for the service on a monthly basis. The corporations would be relieved of the burden of buying and managing the technology.

The vision appealed to customers and investors alike. Hayden, who co-founded *Magellan*, one of the Net's first search engines, began lining up Critical Path's first customers that October. By mid-1998, the company had pocketed $17mn in backing from venture-capital firms, including Benchmark Capital and Mohr, Davidow Ventures. Critical Path also received funding from Internet heavyweights E*Trade Group Inc. and Network Solutions Inc., both of which would become cornerstone customers. In just 15 months, a small band of geeks had built what was suddenly one of the Internet's most promising companies.

Hickey's background, however, could have raised some eyebrows. In his previous job at GlobalCenter, he had succeeded as a short-term specialist – rapidly expanding the company's business before selling it 19 months later. He pushed his sales team to reach roughly $25mn in 1997 sales. He then raised the goal to $60mn for 1998, the forecast upon which GlobalCenter would eventually be sold. In fact, according to former GlobalCenter executives, sales ultimately totalled just $48mn in 1998. His critics say that his lofty projections helped GlobalCenter fetch more money in the sale. And if a buyer had not surfaced in time, the company's prospects might have been damaged. Global Crossing, which now owns Frontier, declined to comment.

Just five months into his tenure at Critical Path, in March 1999, Hickey got his chance to shine. His knack for winning over Wall Street analysts and investors would propel Critical Path's blockbuster IPO, when the stock price more than doubled on the first day of trading. Overnight, the company that had racked up just $900,000 in sales the previous year was valued at a staggering $2.5bn.

The jolt of publicity created by the IPO helped the company grow faster. Within months, it had struck deals with British Telecom and Sprint to provide e-mail services for their customers. Critical Path began using its stock for acquisitions, paying $20mn in June 1999 for e-mail provider Fabrik Connect and its 500 customers. Revenues jumped from $70,000 in 1998's first quarter to $1mn in 1999's first quarter. It was a glorious period for Hickey and his team, who had delivered exactly what the board and investors had hoped for.

With his hand firmly on the wheel, Hickey started looking for a quick pay-off. Publicly, he set the goal of bringing to profitability by the fourth quarter of 2000 a company that had lost $117mn in 1999. Privately, he began looking for a potential buyer. Among the numerous companies Hickey approached were Internet software makers Verisign and Inktomi. Hickey's initial asking price, say the execs, was $100 per share, some $5bn in total. It was a hefty premium for a company that was trading at about $70 a share, but in those days of unbridled optimism, a soon-to-be profitable Internet company could command it. "I had no idea he was trying to sell the company," says Hayden.

By September 2000, the situation was looking grim. The collapse of dotcom funding and the financial problems of telecom companies struck hard at two of Critical Path's biggest customer groups. To counterbalance growing expenses, Hickey was pushing his internal sales target up by $2–3mn – to $60mn. And Hickey continued to promise profitability by the fourth quarter.

It was looking less and less as though Critical Path would find a suitor to save it. Hickey had received lukewarm interest from companies such as Verisign, but nobody would even come near his asking price. With the gloomy economy tightening the pursestrings at most tech companies, Critical Path's chances of selling would only get slimmer. "I was always thinking: 'If we can just keep the wheels on this thing for one more month, or one more quarter. Just until we can get it sold,'" recalls a former executive of the company.

By early December, achieving the sales and profit goals was looking impossible, say former executives. Revenues from some acquisitions were coming in well under expectations. For instance, collaboration-software maker docSpace, acquired in March 2000 for $258mn in stock, had projected $3mn in 2000 sales when it was purchased. In reality, it would deliver revenues of just $300,000, according to a former executive.

Critical Path made a last sales blitz. But in January 2001, instead of the profit long promised by the company's management, Critical Path posted a loss of 16 cents a share. Then the unwinding really started. On February 2, the company suspended two top executives and started an internal investigation into its financial practices after questions arose about the way executives reported revenue from several sales contracts. The Securities and Exchange Commission began an investigation, the stock plunged, and Wall Street analysts and investors began accusing Critical Path of deliberately cooking its books under heavy pressure to turn a profit.

The company was eventually forced to restate its financial results from the third and fourth quarters of 2000, lowering its annual revenue by 13 percent and widening its loss by more than a third. The board forced out the chief executive, the president and the vice president for worldwide sales and dismissed eight members of the sales team.

After the scandal broke, the board appointed venture capitalist William E. McGlashan as chief executive to help company founder David Hayden turn the business around. They cut staff levels in half and shut down the company's weaker operations, many of which emerged as a result of various acquisitions. The company is now refocusing on its original core business of e-mail systems and data management. The next challenge is winning back the confidence of investors and customers alike.

What had started as a dream of building the Internet future ended up a cynical exercise in seeking quick profits. "I just don't think they realized that they were playing with other people's money," says one of Critical Path's burned shareholders. That could be an epitaph not just for Critical Path and other dotcoms but for many participants in the bull market of the late 1990s.

The Global Dimension

- » Capital flows wherever it finds the best investment opportunities.
- » Private equity investing in emerging markets.
- » Lessons learned.

Globalization, so the theory goes, means that capital flows wherever it finds the best investment opportunities. The end of the Bretton Woods system that kept exchange rates fixed signaled the rebirth of the global capital market. Reductions in trade barriers and the falling costs of computers and communications has driven the increased flow of goods and money around the globe. The reality for business has been rather more prosaic.

In practice, globalization has been mixed blessing for most companies. It has added to the pressures on sprawling conglomerates to restructure at the same time as providing the freer flow of capital that enables the restructuring to take place. It has led to unprecedented numbers of mergers and acquisitions, while giving a boost to enterprise. It has brought new challenges to companies attempting to realize their investments and given a boost to the exit route of choice for many conglomerates, the management buy-out.

Before the 1990s, equity imvesting in developing markets was a tiny part of most companies' portfolios. During the past decade, foreign direct investment increased three times as fast as output. Overall, according to the *Economist*, half of all foreign direct investment now involves mergers and acquisitions.

The increased liquidity that the freer flow of capital around the world's financial centers produces has also given a lift to enterprise in emerging markets. Charles Jonscha of Central European Trust, the investment banking specialist, estimates that foreign direct investment accounts for around 30% of portfolio investments in the stock markets in Czechoslovakia and Poland, where his company does most of its business.[1]

He says that the main impact of foreign investment has been to boost liquidity in financial transactions. This in turn, he says, has helped to stimulate entrepreneurship. With more money around, local entrepreneurs have set their sights on bigger deals. For example, Kulzyka Holdings, run by Jerzi Kulzyka, one of Poland's high-profile entrepreneurs, got together recently with France Telecom to buy a 30% stake in Poland's privatized telecommunications company.

A less obvious effect has been the raising of standards and expectations of the local business community. Investment banks, says Jonscha, now have to pay higher salaries to retain young executives.[1] The capital markets of the ex-Communist states, it seems, are beginning to display some of the same symptoms of those of North America and Western Europe.

But it is by no means certain that all emerging markets will develop along the same lines as the West. Political leaders pay lip service to the doctrine of joining the move towards free trade and open markets, but the reality is sometimes very different. Some cultures may never conform to the Western idea of the market. If cultural convergence does come about, it may well occur around the clan-like networks characteristic of Asian cultures rather than the impersonal relationships implied by the Western idea of the market. Why should a huge economy like China throw away a successful business model when it has turned in one of the highest growth rates in the world since the 1980s?

What Western entrepreneurs and investors have to remember is that emerging markets, especially those of the Third World are, by definition, relatively rudimentary. Their inefficiencies present opportunities, for sure, but their structures present additional obstacles to foreigners, above and beyond the usual risks.

Even after overcoming the obstacles to make a successful investment, there are additional difficulties in exiting and realizing your return.

IPOs are rarer, more complex, and often involve far lower trading volumes, resulting in less liquid equity markets. The prospect of selling to a local buyer is often limited by the concentration of wealth among a relatively small pool of potential buyers. Select groups of wealthy families frequently dominate the financial institutions. There is a less well-developed venture capital industry and equity capital is concentrated in fewer hands.

All of this strongly suggests there is a clear case for looking before you leap. Western companies have to understand the additional uncertainties surrounding ventures into emerging markets. They need to look for higher rates of return to compensate for the higher risks.

The good news is that there are a number of signs pointing to a more favorable climate for emerging market investors.

» Globalization continues to lower barriers to cross-border investment and increase the importance of the private sector for development.
» The proliferation of indigenous new economy companies has raised the awareness of local entrepreneurs of the value of outside investors.

» Pools of local savings are expanding rapidly, and local institutional investors are increasingly likely to allocate a portion of their portfolios to private equity.
» Local professional talent is expanding rapidly.
» The economic indicators in both Latin America and Asia suggest a period of strong growth.

There is also ample opportunity to capitalize on the early experience of others to develop an approach that will enhance performance.

EQUITY INVESTMENTS IN EMERGING MARKETS

One common refrain is that the private equity industry is too new for a meaningful performance evaluation. Predictably, exits have been slow to materialize, according to this view, but will accelerate as time passes. Although true, this explanation is probably unconvincing to institutional investors who are under pressure to perform, and have alternative investment opportunities.

Unfortunate timing is a second explanation. US and European private equity funds have been experiencing unprecedented returns until recently, which exaggerate their performance relative to emerging market funds. However, there are signs that spreads between the two fund categories will narrow, demonstrating once again the industry's cyclical nature.

LESSONS FROM EARLY EXPERIENCE

Looking back at the origins and early growth of the private equity industry, most funds replicated the US venture capital model almost in its entirety. There was some recognition of the distinctions between industrialized and emerging market investment climates, but the prevailing view was that the similarities far outweighed the differences. The emerging market funds, therefore, were strikingly similar in terms of legal structure, fund raising strategy, fee structure, professional staffing, the approach to deal origination, due diligence, valuation, and most importantly, exit strategy.

In fact, early stage experience suggests that private equity investing in emerging markets is a fundamentally different business than in the US and Europe. For example, some commentators have pointed out that western methods of valuation are inappropriate for emerging markets, which may not price risk adequately. Fund operating costs also tend to be higher and all aspects of corporate governance, are not only different but vastly more complicated.

Of greatest significance, exiting investments in most developing countries is an entirely different and more complex process. These fundamental differences suggest that the original model must be adjusted to better reflect emerging market realities. There are a number of specific lessons.

Go local

In virtually every aspect of the business, stronger local presence is likely to reduce costs and enhance operating performance. Market intelligence, from deal origination to exit, is likely to improve, as will effective post-investment involvement.

Adjust the profile of targeted companies

Avoid traditional, family-owned companies unless there are clear signs that local owners are willing and able to conform to international standards of corporate governance and integrity, and early agreement can be reached on an acceptable exit strategy. New economy companies tend to have fewer unacceptable business practices, less hidden liabilities, and managers who are more "modern "and flexible.

Mobilize local government support

More effective collaboration with local government and business leaders can instigate changes that would enhance industry performance, such as corporate governance reform, minority shareholder rights, tax treatment, and the dissemination of information on international best practices.

Think creatively about exit strategies

The IPO route has proven to be a flawed strategy in most developing countries, which has consequences for virtually every aspect of the business. This suggests that public market comparisons are not appropriate benchmarks for valuation.

The issue of exit must be realistically assessed in detail before investing. For example, if an IPO is not realistic, a determination that must be made early in the process, prospective strategic buyers must be identified, along with the auction potential. Agreement must be reached on specific value enhancements, how they will be achieved, and when. And there must be a consensus on the post-investment role of the fund.

NOTE

1 Charles Jonscha, personal interview, August 2001.

The State of the Art

» Don't get on the down escalator.
» Investment pipeline adds value.
» Strategic and financial returns.

"It's harder to get out of deals than to get into deals. Anybody can put money in the company. Not everyone can grow a company, make it interesting and sell it on."

Will Schmidt, Advent International

WHAT INHIBITS EXIT PLANNING?

You'd expect the notion of an exit, the path to realizing the gains from an investment, to loom large in any plans for a growing business enterprise. But that has by no means always been the case. Venture capitalists even have a word for companies that get stuck in the portfolio that nobody wants; they're called the "living dead."

Some entrepreneurs set out consciously to build up a business with the express intention to sell out at the earliest opportunity. Many Internet entrepreneurs had an IPO in mind almost before they had registered a company name, for example. In the classic turnaround situation, a businessman buys a failing company, works hard to sort out its problems and return it to profitability with a view to realizing an immediate short-term gain. An astute management team contemplating a buy-out will aim to strike the deal at a low point in the business' performance, before realizing large gains following a startling improvement or economic upturn.

Indeed there is a special strain of proactive investor who is motivated exclusively by the prospect of exiting an investment profitably, measuring success by the speed and size of a cash return, measured by the IRR (internal rate of return) from a project.

But the evidence is that on the whole, the process is somewhat more haphazard. Many entrepreneurs – perhaps the majority – set out to establish and run a business without much thought to an eventual outcome. The family-run business is a particular case in point, where the founder's expectation is that successive generations will continue to run the business – even if it does not work out quite as the founder might have hoped. In a private company, owner-managers may not be in a position to make a decision to sell, as they may be required to give first option to existing shareholders that may be unwilling or unable to buy.

And while there are certainly many proactive investors, there are plenty of reactive investors, too. They may be informal investors who are content to sit back as long as the interest or dividends keep coming in, or business angels driven as much by their desire to apply their know-how to a fledgling company as they are to think about realizing an exit.

They may even be professional venture capitalists, genuinely concerned not to jeopardize the long-term prospects of a company by pushing for an early sale or flotation. A reputation for over-zealousness in that direction may not be to their advantage and, anyway, buyers will probably discount the price they are prepared to pay if they know that there is a keen seller. Other VCs may be relying on the company directors or other shareholders to call the timing of an exit, when they judge the timing is optimal.

Managers of a growing company may, themselves, be the chief obstacles. They may well resist an exit, especially if the main prospect is a trade sale. For them, a trade sale could mean loss of independence or autonomy. Their venture backers, the professional venture capital specialists, face a big challenge in providing incentives and motivation in this situation.

"Obviously, you can't sell a business without the management team's consent," says Chris Hemmings who heads up European private equity business for Pricewaterhousecoopers, "so persuasion is the order of the day." It's rare, asserts Hemmings, to find a management team that's against the notion of an exit, in principle. The main argument, he says, is usually over timing.

The institutional investor, says Hemmings, will generally have a view about the best time to maximize the price of a sale or a flotation. Quite often, a potential buyer will make a pre-emptive bid for a company in the run-up to a flotation. But the management team will consider it's still too early.

"In most cases, there's a rational discussion and it's all fairly amicable" says Hemmings. But now and again, he says, there's "shades of 'over my dead body'." It's situations like those, he says, that create the pressure for secondary buy-outs, where a financial buyer, usually another venture capitalist, buys out the original investor. This means the management team can remain in control of their firm's destiny. Another solution, says Hemmings, is to dangle the carrot of the sale proceeds provocatively. Surprisingly, they may not have made the calculation for themselves.

"Very few sit down and calculate what their equity is worth," he says, "they're focused on the profit from the business." In nine out of ten situations, says Hemmings, when the team understands how big their share of the proceeds would be, they'd go for it.

INCREASED INTEREST IN EXIT PLANNING

Like many in the industry, Hemmings says there's an increasing interest in exit planning, as the market becomes more sophisticated. It is all part of the process at his firm.

"Now, we'll do a proper study of the exit potential, he says. This will cover whether there should be an IPO, where a trade buyer might come from and how soon the business will be ready for a disposal. Then, he says, "we'll start monitoring the plan and driving the management to achieve it."

His colleague John Wall agrees that the industry is rapidly becoming more sophisticated. He says:

"It's matured a lot. More deals, bigger deals, more experience. Financial buyers are now more dominant in the marketplace. They have access to vast amounts of capital – billion dollar funds are common now. They're more sophisticated, operating with much larger amounts, lots of money, they've learned from their past mistakes as well."

Wall, a past board member of the EVCA Exits Committee in Brussels, says exit planning was less usual only a few years ago:

"It was astonishing how many VCs were going into deals without having defined their exit strategy. What you find now is you've moved into more of an institutional buy-out market and the VCs are thinking about the strategy for disposal even before they've bought the company.

"They're not even bothering to go to the auction unless they know how they're going to sell it."

MANAGING THE BUSINESS FOR EXIT

Venture capitalists, it seems, have tended in the past to be better at investing than exiting. The net result is a slow-moving pipeline of risk capital backed investment projects: if you took a snapshot of the total pipeline, you would probably see more activity at the end where new companies are coming into the pipeline than dropping off at the other end. It's this excess which John Wall and Julian Smith, of Pricewaterhousecoopers, call the *investment overhang*.

Wall and Smith suggest that it would do no harm at all for investors and entrepreneurs to explicitly consider an exit strategy from the earliest stage of an investment relationship.

There may be circumstances beyond anyone's control which make it necessary to change an exit plan – the postponement of an IPO due to unfavorable market conditions is an obvious example. And exit planning is not a cure-all for every aspect of business performance. But the advantages of thinking about an exit, for example more focused decision-making, will generally be of benefit to the day-to-day management of a company.

The most important thing about exit strategies is to have one in the first place. It is vitally important for entrepreneurs and investors to have a shared view of the investment horizon and the way value is to be realized.

The time to introduce an exit strategy, say Smith and Wall, is at the earliest stages of an investment relationship, as part of the due diligence process in the case of professional investors, like venture capital companies.

The way to introduce it, if the management team is not keen to think about it, according to the authors, is by asking them to consider what would happen to the business in the event of the retirement or death of one of the team. Or whether they might want to buy back the investor's shares at some stage.

The overall aim is to line up the interests of the managers of the new enterprise and the investors. Or – as that is not always possible – to have some clearly stated objectives agreed for the life of the investment.

BENEFITS OF EXIT PLANNING

Chief amongst the objectives is the preferred exit route. One of the strongest arguments for planning for an IPO is that the effort it takes to promote the company for a flotation will often winkle out a trade buyer anxious to make a pre-emptive bid. This puts the shareholders in the comfortable position of being able to choose between two options; the higher return that an IPO often delivers, together with continued control of the existing management team of the company; or the speed, simplicity, and lower cost of a trade sale, where there's only one customer to worry about.

Selecting the preferred exit route and defining the likely buyer for the new company gives a useful reference against which to test whether the business is heading in the right direction. Are the business strategy and structure likely to bring about the desired exit? Are the managers keen to exit or do they need to be offered incentives?

There are other benefits from thinking through the exit strategy that repay the effort. Smith and Wall recommend drawing up a checklist for the management team to consider each aspect of exit preparation (see below). For example, one shareholder can hold up the disposal of a business. Keeping the shareholding structure from the start will avoid this situation arising.

Thinking about the exit strategy can also raise the potential value of a disposal. By getting inside the mind of a potential buyer, says Hemmings, it's sometimes possible to achieve a better outcome. It's not always obvious what value the opportunity represents to a potential buyer. Hemmings gives an example of a transaction that PCW advised on a few years ago, involving the purchase of a site owned by Belfast City Airport for $32mn. "We sold it to a property company two years later for $100mn – on the basis of its property value," says Hemmings. "The shareholders made an absolute fortune."

EXIT CHECKLIST[1]

Things for management to consider to enhance the business and make exit easier.

Strategy
» Have one!
» Try to achieve a consistent growth record.
» Reflect exit plans in the timing and choice of strategy options.

» Ensure that new opportunities are being created as old ones are realized – to ensure that growth continues.

» Remember that competitors may be the likely purchasers – they will pay more for a business, which can be merged to provide profit improvements. If they do not buy, their interest will increase the price.

PR/marketing

» All achievements should be reported in trade and financial press.
» Results and new orders should always be announced.
» Remember that advertising and marketing does not just sell the product – it may help sell the business.

Financial statements

» Accounts should look professional and be well presented from the first year.
» They should be informative, and reflect the strategy of the business – they are not just a legal requirement.
» Ensure they are consistent from year to year.

Reporting systems

» Management of the business and exit are both facilitated by reliable, timely, and relevant management information.
» These requirements should be addressed from day one.

Legal structure

» Keep it simple. If it is not, simplify it while there is time.
» Avoid minority stakes which do not have a strategic purpose – or try to eliminate them prior to exit. One single shareholder can hold up the whole process.

Management

» Ensure the team is balanced, experienced, and of a high caliber.
» Do not allow gaps to develop.

» Plan for succession.
» Ensure they can individually demonstrate a successful record at exit.

CREATIVE EXITS

Exit strategies are a necessary, yet under-researched and under-discussed stage of private equity firms' business, says Christopher Mackenzie, a partner at Clayton, Dubilier & Rice in London. Funds have so many ways to extract value from investments, but it is important to establish early on how that value will be realized

Says MacKenzie:

"I do not know why that is, because it is such a huge part of the economic equation. Most of the private equity community take the view 'if I improve profitability and reduce costs, the business will be more valuable and someone will want to buy it.' People also say there is no point trying to settle the exit strategy at the point of investment because they do not know what the markets will be, so any discussion is a waste of time. I disagree."

Yet private equity firms at times have to be flexible. Clayton Dubilier has been creative with its investment in Remington Arms, which it bought from DuPont in late 1993 for $300mn. Since then, Remington's profits have increased, and the company's annual cash flow is now $75mn – greater than the firm's initial equity investment of $70mn. The investment now spins off a 100% cash return on its equity investment, since the debt is almost completely paid off. Even so, no one wants to buy it, because the company is wrongly perceived as a handgun manufacturer, Mackenzie says. Companies that make handguns face potential liability lawsuits in the US. Even though Remington makes shotguns and military weapons and has diversified into fishing line and accessories, "you can not float it to save your life," says Mackenzie.

Instead, Clayton Dubilier still owns the company and has increased its debts to pay dividends to investors. This year the company will pay $50mn of dividends, says Mackenzie. However, he adds that "within two years all investors will get their money back, and then some." He reckons that Clayton Dubilier's return on investment averages 44%. Small to mid-sized company stock offerings are not as attractive to institutional investors as larger ones, says Ned Gilhuly, managing director of Kohlberg Kravis Roberts in London. He says that

> "There are fewer people managing more money, and they are not very interested in small to midcap companies unless they have really exciting growth prospects. That means private equity investors need to focus on companies with strong growth or they must focus on a trade sale exit."

That is one reason Cinven sold Comax to Amey, a competitor, rather than floating it, says John Brown, deputy managing director at Cinven.

Cinven had thought a float would be the best exit for the business, but it received an attractive offer from Amey, which it accepted.

Amey, which had been moving away from its construction business, transformed itself by buying Comax from Cinven for £86mn, plus £59mn of debt, in July 1999. Comax specializes in providing support services in secure environments. Cinven bought it from the government's defense research agency for about £74mn two years earlier.

DOES EXIT PLANNING REALLY MAKE A DIFFERENCE?

There is surprisingly little research on the effect that having an explicit exit strategy has on the investment performance of a growth business. However, some research by Steven N. Kaplan and Per Strömberg suggests that the venture capitalist's initial appraisal of an investment is a good predictor of performance (see Chapter 8 for details).

But only in some specific respects: they find that the quality of the management team, competition, and strategy are related to subsequent performance; but the appraiser's assessment of market attractiveness and market size risk are unrelated to that performance.

More controversially, venture capitalists may, it seems, be more effective at influencing the value of their investments at the other end of the process – at payback time.

Joshua Lerner, a professor at Harvard Business School, has studied the effects of distribution policies on the returns that venture capitalists make to their partners when investment funds mature. He concludes that venture capitalists have an incentive to time the distribution of fund proceeds to maximize their own compensation. Their inside knowledge of their portfolio firms, he suggests, would enable them to work out when the share price has peaked, timing the distribution accordingly.

Similarly, they have an incentive to maximize the apparent value of returns from the fund. This is the most important marketing tool when it comes to raising money for a new fund. Lerner provides a convincing account, based on his analysis of more than 750 distribution deals, showing how VCs can time the distribution to suit them (see Chapter 8 for details).

ALIGNING THE OBJECTIVES

There is a great deal of discussion in venture capital circles about distinguishing between strategic investment and investments that are strictly financial. The bottom-line test says you shouldn't be investing at all unless you're aiming to make loads of money – preferably bucket-loads. According to Will Schmidt of Advent International, the venture capital specialist, understanding this simple rule is one of the keys to developing a successful relationship between entrepreneur and investor.

"Exit to make an outrageous financial gain," advises Schmidt – "that's rule number one in venture capital and should be rule number one of corporate venturing. Otherwise you shouldn't necessarily be thinking about an equity stake."

In corporate venturing, particularly, there is scope for mixing the aims of an investment program. For example, at least part of the aim could be to acquire, say, access to developing technology, through a stake in a technically advanced start-up. But, says Schmidt, there is no reason for these aims to be mutually exclusive.

"There used to be this feeling that strategic and financial objectives for a corporate were inversely correlated. But that's total rubbish. You want the technology and the company to be outrageously successful. A corporate is going to want to partner with somebody that's successful in the marketplace. So in fact the history is that it's highly correlated, when you're talking about real corporate venturing.

"Frankly, if they are inversely correlated, in other words it's a niche company with a special technology, then it's a lousy venture deal. The corporate probably doesn't want to put equity into it. Buy license rights. Do something else to get access to the technology. But don't put an equity investment in a company that is not going to be outrageously successful."

Clarifying the overall aim is one thing. But agreeing on the detail is key to the success of the relationship. Part of the exit strategy is to try to anticipate potential sources of conflict in advance. It's all a matter of aligning those objectives.

"Thinking about exit is pretty important," says Schmidt, ... "so is aligning those sets of objectives between investor and management ... Don't mix objectives." For example a corporate venture program can have any one of a number of objectives. At one end of the spectrum, the corporate could be buying into a company they want to eventually acquire. At the other extreme it might take a minority stake in a company in whose technology they're interested. In between there's an investment to cement some sort of rights: product rights for a biotech company; exclusive rights to market somebody's software, or technology license rights for your core product. In each case, the objectives are very different.

"On one hand he doesn't care what happens to the company" explains Schmidt, "he just wants to make an outrageous financial gain. On the other hand he wants it. Then in the middle, he may not want it but he sure as heck doesn't want it to go to a competitor."

It's in these cases where the corporate venture team wants to control the exit or wants to acquire the company that problems can potentially arise with a general venture capitalist.

"We want to have a free auction," explains Schmidt; "to sell the company to whoever pays for it, unless there's been something pre-negotiated. That's why you have to make sure there's an alignment of interest in the syndicate."

At the heart of it all is doing what's best for the enterprise. To some, equity means ownership: "I own this thing; nobody else should have a piece of it, its mine." That mentality may keep it yours but it won't necessarily let the company sing.

DRIVING TO AN IPO

The attractions of an IPO are numerous. The increased exposure and visible valuation of publicly listed companies gives them a better standing among the investment community, which is a great help for further rounds of financing. Publicly traded shares provide the increased liquidity that enable early investors to cash in their investment and the chance to reward employees through stock options. The respectability that a listing confers can even gain a company better trading terms.

Will Schmidt of Advent International confirms the value of planning for an IPO in building the business. "Driving to an IPO is usually a good thing," he says. "Because you require robust management; you require international accounting standards; you require a solid management team. It's getting the business in shape whatever the outcome."

However, although everyone dreams of the IPO, especially in the technology sector space, they only account for around 20–30% of exits, far less than trade sales. As Schmidt points out, it's important to look beyond the seductive quality of the IPO to the real needs of the business.

"It's a kind of great flag on the hill that you want to take when you're involved in investment," says Schmidt. "On the other hand, if you realize that an IPO might not be the best thing, you probably want to be on board to drive the company. It might be that designing to go public on NASDAQ is not going to optimize value. You might decide what you really want to do is to invest to become the leader in France – only – to be a plump rabbit to sell to some other acquirer."

That would have the advantage of avoiding the overheads of an IPO, which are onerous: massive public scrutiny, the large cost of the underwriting, legal and accounting activities and the management time spent managing the whole process of road shows and analyst briefings.

TELLING THE IPO STORY

There's a sense of excitement about a successful flotation. A decent track record and cashflow are simply prerequisites for a successful IPO. It's the anticipation of high returns in the future that sparks the interest. Telling a good story in the lead-up to a flotation is an essential part of capturing the fancy of the public.

Timing the investment is also crucial. It will take a typical company a series of three or four rounds of funding to go public. The "A" round gets a product to market; rounds "B" and "C" are to expand market penetration; "D" – pre-IPO – is to boost the balance sheet and prepare to present to the IPO community.

LIVING WITH THE INVESTMENT CYCLE

The state of the IPO (initial public offering) market is the main factor in determining the likely return to investors and, hence, the availability of money for new enterprises. Even a good business with a good track record, with good management will find it quite difficult to raise any money when the IPO market is flat.

The one thing to remember, says Jos Peeters, founder of Capricorn Venture Partners, a Belgian-based venture capital specialist and member of the exits committee of EVCA, the European Venture Capital Association, is that IPO markets are very cyclical.

"They come and they go," says Peeters "and they come and they go for sectors. At the moment [December 2001] it's tough for everybody. But remember there were times that you couldn't bring a biotech company public, but you could almost sell a dog with a GSM on his neck. Then there are times like now when nothing in the telecom sector works, but there's still some appetite for biotech."

The markets in the USA normally lead the cycle. "Europe tends to lag behind," says Peeters. "The bubble arrived a bit late and when we started to see the decline, the USA was already recovering. It's a little less volatile in Europe but the patterns are very similar." The Internet frenzy and boom in technology stocks had the effect of shortening the period for new companies to come to market.

"Time scales were shortening," says Peeters. "Month by month time scales were shortening between creating a company and going public.

It was a trend, but that's over now. At the moment they are stretched out again. That's one of the uncertainties in the venture – the private equity – world, which creates a reluctance to do deals. You don't know how long you will have to finance a company before it can go to the public market. There's a lot of uncertainty now. There was probably a more typical 5-7 year period in the early to mid 1990s. That contracted to 3 years at the end of the decade. Now you don't know, but it's more likely to be somewhere in between."

The rise and fall of the investment cycle is compounded by people's tendency to follow the trend, says Peeters, something the technology sector has illustrated very clearly.

"Investors behave a little like sheep," he says. "They all turn away from a sector, together. If you compare the strength of NASDAQ versus the NYSE you see that NASDAQ is undervalued compared to the Dow Jones and that hasn't been the case for three or four years." Peeters is convinced there will be an upswing in technology stocks and that investors, once again, will return to invest in unison. The uncertainty, of course, is when it will take place.

"Everybody knows what will happen, the only question is when will it happen" says Peeters. "Technology is not dead. Technology will be a strong performing sector in the coming years but will it start tomorrow or in three months or in a year – that's more difficult to judge.

The cyclical factor also has a big impact on market valuations, says Peeters. When the markets are buoyant, he says, like they were 18 months ago, many companies take their chance well prepared or ill prepared, they see a window and jump. It's only afterwards that some buyers find out that what they bought wasn't exactly what they thought they were buying. Add to that that generally because the valuations are highly dependent on market prospects, on revenue prospects, and if anything in the past year we've had the scaling back of forecasts. That has a dramatic impact on future valuations.

It's tough, of course, to go against the herd. It's a bold corporate venturing manager, for example, that continues to invest when the markets are flat, even when in theory that's exactly what he or she should be doing, in order to snap up a bargain. Following the slump in Internet and technology stocks, there are few corporate venturing programs that are maintaining their momentum. Cisco Systems stands out as an exception, but many more, like the indebted European PTTs, have cut their programs severely.

Will Schmidt of Advent International, the venture capital and corporate venturing specialists, agrees that corporates are not immune from the collective, short-term view.

"The corporate appetite is often correlated with the fact that the IPO market is shut and times are tough," says Schmidt. "It takes a real long term view – and a good one – to say 'go for it' when the rest of senior management is dying at analysts meetings trying to explain their earnings shortfall."

Schmidt warns against simply doing deals to take advantage of short-term trends like the Internet frenzy or a bullish stock market. He advises that the aim of venture investing is to build a real business that has genuine synergies with your own operating activities. A decision to exit should not be driven by the state of the IPO market.

"Well, if it's a good company in a good sector and you can't go public now, just wait," advises Schmidt. "Just grow the company and wait. Is the IPO market open? No, well you have a choice: you either wait or look for a trade sale. It sounds simplistic, but it is that simple in a standard transaction."

Sitting tight is an option, perhaps, if you have the resources you need. The thing to remember is that an IPO is not an exit event, in itself, it's a capital raising exercise. The real problem in a flat IPO market is not that you can't go public, but that you can't raise funds.

Not quite so much of a problem if you're already generating sufficient quantities of cash. Companies that are cash flow positive can afford to take longer to raise money, as they are not under any particular pressure. But if you can't go public and the company is still cash flow negative, you've got to get the thing funded somehow.

Venture capitalists that usually provide the successive rounds of funding that it takes to get a new company to market grow even more cautious in difficult times. But there is a usually a point where their greed overcomes their caution. As Peeters warns: "Those that are under pressure might have to review their valuations downward to get investors in."

The difference when things are buoyant is that a company has an option to go public. The expectation of an IPO often produces a better exit price. As Peeters points out, many IPOs are pulled days before a company would have gone public because somebody has suddenly appeared and makes a better.

"Many companies have gone public to put themselves in the shop window" he says. "Look, here we are, aren't we beautiful, and by the way we're only this price. Along comes a larger corporation and says I need those goodies, but I'll have to pay a premium, otherwise I don't get them."

As ever, it's always much easier to negotiate from a position of strength, which you do when you are confident: that you can go to the market or sit tight as you have your own independent growth path.

NOTE

1 Taken from Wall, John and Smith, Julian (1997) "Better exits: a survey of the practical experience of major European venture capital funds in exiting their investments," EVCA; and author's personal interviews with Chris Hemmings, Jos Peeters, Will Schmidt and John Wall, September/October 2001.

Exit Strategies in Practice: Success Stories

» Apple Computer: It started with a chip, then Apple's corporate venture with ARM Holdings returns big time.
» Delifrance Asia: Singapore fast bakery franchise IPO. An entrepreneur takes the French café concept into Asia and builds a 15-country franchise operation, country by country.
» Freeserve: The Internet Service Provider IPO/trade sale. John Pluthero masterminds Dixons' pioneering spin-off

This chapter provides a number of case studies, showing exit strategies in practice.

APPLE'S CORPORATE VENTURE WITH ARM HOLDINGS RETURNS BIG TIME[1]

Enterprise: ARM Holdings
Investor: Apple Computer
Exit strategy: stock sale, following IPO
Payback: For a stake of $2.5mn in 1996, Apple has recouped more than $800mn to date (December 2001)

It's been called the greatest corporate venture of all time. For Apple's investment of $2.5mn in ARM Holdings, the computer chip designer and the UK's most successful technology company has recouped them $800mn. Yet Apple ended up with a stake in ARM by luck rather than any belief they were backing a winner. "The only reason Apple invested in ARM was because of the Newton project," says Larry Tesler, former Apple chief scientist and member of ARM's board.

Newton was an early attempt at the "personal digital assistant" market, the Palm Pilot of its day. Apple's team working on the Newton had been around for a few years when Tesler joined in 1989 to turn the project around. They'd been having trouble winning support for a launch within the company.

The problem, says Tesler, was the fact that the Newton was going to be priced at $7000. The engineers had let the price spiral out of control because they were racing to create the first and best pocket computer with handwriting recognition. "But a lot of what they were doing was science for its own sake not because it met any customer needs," says Tesler.

Tesler realized Apple would never launch a pocket computer at a price above $1000. He made a dramatic price cut by changing the chip set. There were three processors in the Newton prototype – two from AT&T and an ARM chip from Acorn Computers. The AT&T chips cost $40 each while the ARM chips cost $20 each. In addition Newton was paying AT&T $1mn a year towards chip development. Tesler persuaded the engineers to settle for a single processor.

"Instead of having almost $100 worth of chips in this thing why not have one ARM chip and make it the main processor," he told them.

However Apple wasn't keen on buying chips from a supplier like Acorn, which it saw as a rival. Tesler mentioned this to VLSI Technology, who manufactured the processor chips for Acorn. They said "we've been trying to spin ARM out of Acorn for a year but we couldn't find another investor. All that's needed is a couple of million dollars." Tesler's contact at VLSI suggested he get in touch with Herman Hauser at Acorn.

Hauser had been involved with ARM chip development since the beginning, in 1985. In fact it was Hauser who had named the chips Advanced RISC Machines or ARM for short. Hauser saw enormous potential in these microprocessors and had been trying to spin out the chip designers so they could develop products for other computer manufacturers. With VLSI already onboard Hauser had been looking for a third investor. Then Tesler came along.

The negotiations took place at a time when Apple was rethinking its investment criteria. The board turned the proposition down flat.

"It was an immediate no," says Tesler, "this isn't the kind of thing that we do any more." Despite turning him down, Dan Isler, Apple's head of corporate investment, encouraged Tesler to pursue the proposition with Advent International, the venture capitalists. Advent proved helpful at developing a new business model

ARM would make no physical product. Instead they would design and develop microprocessors, then license their designs to partner companies, who would manufacture the actual chips and incorporate them into products. ARM would then receive royalty payments for every chip produced. This was a brilliant new concept. "Selling intellectual property was not really being done yet," says Tesler.

Tesler went back to the Apple board to ask for the financing needed to get ARM spun out. In preparation his corporate investment, colleagues coached him on the pitch.

"They said I should forget all the stuff Advent told us about the business model because it wasn't really going to work," remembers Tesler.

"You should just say that the Newton project needs the chip - fast," they told him. "And that it wasn't safe to get it directly from Acorn. And that for a one time investment of $2.5mn we would get this chip rather than spending $5mn for the AT&T chips every year."

Again the board was inclined to say "no" to the investment. They feared a little company like ARM would be wiped out by competition like Motorola, Intel, and NTT. "They just didn't think it was going to happen," says Tesler. But they finally relented on the urgent need for the chip for the Newton project and approved the expenditure as an expense.

"Just make sure they don't go out of business before they deliver you the chip," one board member told Tesler. "After that we don't care."

If Apple was going to invest just to get a chip for Newton, it needed to be a new one. The ARM chip used in the Newton prototype didn't have some of the features they needed nor was it fast enough to use as a main processor. Acorn had new requirements too. However for the sake of the spin-out they agreed ARM should focus on the chip Apple needed first. The designers even promised to develop it within ten months.

They started looking round for someone to head up the team of 12 engineers they were planning to spin out. Both Advent and an independent source at Motorola recommended Robin Saxby, who had been managing director of two other electronic operations. He proved a first rate choice.

ARM was spun out in 1990. For their $2.5mn stake, Apple received a 47% share, Acorn owned another 47% and VLSI, who put in £250,000, got 6%. VLSI was also their first licensee. Tesler, Hauser, and others involved in the ARM spin-out could see that the future was digital and items such as mobile phones and digital televisions would become mass market. This meant there'd be tremendous growth potential for ARM's low-cost, low-power microprocessors.

ARM soon required some extra financial cushioning. "Advent thought we would need to raise some additional capital," says Tesler. "Apple wasn't going to put in any more and Acorn didn't have any more. So Advent asked everyone from venture capitalists to technology companies, using the same pitch they had used with us. They tried their best yet they couldn't find anyone."

ARM finally got that last bit of outside investment from the Japanese venture capitalist firm Nippon Investment and Finance in 1993. "They invested because we were giving Sharp a license for the Newton," says Tesler. "And Sharp took a license because we were getting money from this venture firm. They figured if Sharp was going to take a license they might do okay and vice versa." Other than that nobody would invest, says Tesler. "I am sure a lot of companies we approached would regret their decision today," he says.

Texas Instruments followed Sharp on board as licensees. As one of the top microchip makers, having Texas as a partner gave ARM's credibility a huge boost. "Now we were able to get almost anyone we wanted," says Tesler.

In 1993 Tesler left the Newton team to take on a new role as Apple's chief scientist. He left a few months before the pocket computer was shipped. He admits many things were still wrong with the product. It was an ignominious failure. Three managers later Apple withdrew the product line.

However, Tesler retained his seat on the ARM board. The company was growing steadily by the end of 1994, but apart from Tesler few Apple executives had registered its progress. One day in 1995 Tesler had a visit from a colleague from the corporate finance group, who had been looking through the books and noticed the investment in ARM. "We're still carrying it on our books as an investment, but we wrote it off as an expense in 1990," she told Tesler. "I wanted to delete it, but I just thought I should check with you first that it has gone out of business and then we can write it off."

According to Tesler she was incredulous when he told her ARM was still in business and that he was about to go to the Apple board to ask them to approve a stock option deal for ARM employees. The board, too, was amazed at ARM's progress. Now they backtracked and said this was "an example of what we should be doing."

The ARM IPO

By the mid-1990s ARM was doing well and its management team was really pushing for an IPO. They wanted independence and additional funding to grow even faster. Apple and VLSI were keen too, but Acorn was stalling.

Acorn, itself, was performing poorly by this time but investors were buying Acorn stock because they knew it owned 47% of ARM. Executives worried that as soon as ARM was floated, these investors would invest directly in ARM and dump their Acorn stock. The pro-flotation faction decided the best thing to do was wait. Eventually Acorn would run out of cash and they would go along with it.

In the meantime Tesler says he "had to keep the ARM guys happy or they would all disappear." He had a lot of long personal talks with Saxby and other top management. The message was "we can't wait any more." "I was afraid," Tesler says, "they would go out there and start talking to head hunters about other jobs."

He managed to convince Apple and Acorn to set up a stock option program for them in 1995. "If ARM did not go public by January 1998 then we would buy their stock at a price set independently," says Tesler. "By demanding that provision I was always able to go to ARM management and say don't worry because one day January 1998 will come."

Acorn agreed to this plan because it was another way of putting the IPO off. But when 1997 came around they were worried because they didn't have any money to buy their share of the stock. Apple, too, had worries, says Tesler. "They had enough money to buy their share of the stock, only they didn't want to use the money for that."

With ARM's star rising, a number of large semiconductor companies came along and offered to buy Apple's share in ARM. The Apple CSO at the time Fred Anderson was very new. He received an offer of $50mn, a great profit on a $2.5mn investment. Fortunately Tesler persuaded him to get a valuation which put a value of $80mn to $100mn on the shares. Anderson was very surprised and decided not to sell. Suddenly he too became nervous. If the IPO wasn't done before January 1998 Apple would have to fork out plenty of cash, which was in short supply. He put all his muscle behind ARM's IPO, assigning a team to assist Tesler.

Meantime Acorn was still stalling and trying to figure out a way to avoid the IPO. Finally they said, we're not sure we'll approve it but go ahead with the paperwork.

At this point Tesler left Apple to become a venture capitalist. He had to give up his seat on the ARM board, though Apple continued to consult him about strategy.

Just in the nick of time Acorn took on a new CEO with a fresh perspective. He saw they were in a disastrous situation and needed cash fast. Selling their ARM stock was their only salvation. "Suddenly they wanted to do the IPO right away" says Tesler, "but they had to hold back for a few more months," while ARM was made a PLC.

Saxby immediately invited Tesler to rejoin the board. His first day back on the job was March 4, 1998 at the meeting where ARM became a PLC. "They added two more board seats and gave me one," say Tesler proudly. "I was made non-executive independent director instead of an Apple director. I've been on the board ever since. I have just been re-elected for my second three-year term last year."

The IPO finally went through on 17 April, 1998. Today ARM is in the FTSE 100. "The chips are now being used in mobile phones and that's what's made ARM such a success" says Tesler. "Motorola wouldn't invest in the beginning, nor would they take a license because they said ARM was a competitor. Then recently they took an architecture license and now they are a major source of ARM chips for handheld devices. Intel also took out a license. Just about every major semiconductor company now has a license."

Tesler says, "Apple lost $100mn to $200mn on the Newton project. In the end they made more than that on the ARM stock. That $2.5 million investment yielded more then the loss and that was the irony of it."

After the IPO Apple and Acorn gave up their board seats entirely because they wanted to be able to cash out their shares without any conflicts over insider information. By the end of 1999 Apple had sold about 80% of their shares.

"In 1998 and 1999 when Apple was selling the shares they were in a terrible cash crunch," says Tesler. "I'm not sure they would have made it, without them. At the least, they would have had to have paid a lot higher interest rates on their loan to do it."

Herman Hauser, now a distinguished venture capitalist at Amadeus Partners, says, "Apple sold out a little bit too early. They got a few hundred million for it but if they had hung on to them they would have got a few billion at the peak of the tech stock boom. At the peak, ARM was worth about $10bn. I think at that stage Apple still had 20%. If they had sold at that stage it would have saved them for some time to come."

"As it is, to get a few hundred million return on your investment is exceptional," says Hauser. "It was the most successful corporate investment Apple has ever made."

APPLE'S ARM INVESTMENT MILESTONES

» **1985**: A group of engineers at Acorn develops the World's first commercial RISC processor.
» **1987**: Acorn's ARM processor debuts as the first RISC processor used in a low-cost personal computer.
» **1989**: Larry Tesler joins Apple's Newton project.
» **1990**:
  » Apple (47% share) Acorn (47% share) and VLSI (6% share) enter into a joint venture and spun out ARM.
  » Apple agrees to a $2.5mn investment to get the chip for the Newton.
  » VLSI becomes ARM's first license holder.
» **1993**:
  » As result Nippon Investment and Finance becomes ARM's fourth and final investor for a 5% share.
  » Sharp and Texas Instruments take a license.
» **1995**:
  » ARM management begins pushing for an IPO.
  » Apple and Acorn set up program whereby if the IPO doesn't take place by January 1998 they will buy ARM employee's stock at an independently assessed price.
» **Summer 1997**:
  » First attempt at IPO scuppered by Acorn.
  » Larry Tesler leaves Apple.
» **Autumn 1997**: Acorn's new CEO gives the ARM IPO the green light.
» **March 4, 1998**:
  » ARM is made a PLC as a step towards the IPO.
  » Larry Tesler rejoins the ARM board as a non-executive independent director.
» **April 17, 1998**:
  » ARM flotation is a success.
  » ARM becomes a FTSE 100 company.
  » Apple and Acorn drop to one ARM board member a piece.

> » **1999**: Apple and Acorn give up their seats on the ARM board so they can sell their shares without being accused of insider trading.
> » **May 5, 1999**: Apple sells another 9 million shares of its stake in ARM – the third tranche since the 1998 initial public offering.
> » **2001**:
>> » To date Apple has made an estimated total of $800 million from its ARM shares.
>> » At present count Apple has about 8 million shares left.

DELIFRANCE ASIA[2]

Enterprise: Delifrance Asia
Based: Singapore
Investors: Grands Moulins de Paris, Vilgrain family, Hugues Prince
Exit strategy: IPO, followed by sale of stock

This is the story of an outstanding entrepreneurial talent that took an existing business concept and developed it throughout South East Asia. It is also a story of bold opportunism, culminating in a successful flotation and exit. The sale of Delifrance Asia in 1998, during the Asian economic slump, achieved a surprisingly high return at a time when realizing a return at all was something of a triumph.

The Delifrance concept is to bring a corner of Paris – well, at least the smell and taste of freshly baked croissants and pastries – to aspiring "foodies" the world over.

The key to the business is the way it satisfies a demand for traditional French style bakery, without the cost of traditional French style expertise, premises or staff. Delifrance products are delivered frozen and freshly baked at the point of sale. The method uses techniques developed by the Vilgrain family, which had been involved in the flour milling business in France since the beginning of the century. The frozen technique delays the fermentation and baking process so that staff can "bake off" products, achieving a consistent quality, with the minimum skill.

The Delifrance operation in Singapore started by importing breads from France. Then in 1983, the company was incorporated under the name of Vie de France Singapore, as the international operations of Grands Moulins de Paris, which was at that time controlled by the Vilgrain family. When the Vilgrains wanted to develop the Asian market, they contacted the French embassy in Singapore and were put in touch with Hugues Prince.

Prince comes from a wine brokerage business family in Burgundy. He graduated from ESSEC in France, then did his military service in the French embassy in Singapore for 1.5 years. He joined the GMP group, went back to France for six months then back to Singapore to start up the operation.

"We were independent of the mother-company in most respects," says Prince, "except that most of the shares belonged to the Vilgrain family." Prince became one of the principal stakeholders and operated relatively autonomously.

"We did it on our own in Asia," says Prince. "I was always employed by Vilgrain," he says, "but apart from the occasional visit from the son of the former chairman of GMP, we had little technical support from France. We talked quite often on the phone and we both had an interest in entrepreneurship."

Prince became the main architect of Delifrance's expansion in Asia. "The name and the product existed" says Prince. "We developed the product to an Asian standard. We did things differently."

"In Asia the bread market, especially for French style products, wasn't very big. So we started off with a café concept where consumers could get freshly baked, good quality products at a reasonable. So we didn't really start as a bakery company, which was the origins of the group, but as a café-bakery. It was a 'restaurant rapid.'

"The mentality of the French and Asian people is very similar – food occupies a very important space in their lives [i.e. keen on good quality and high standards]. Food is incredible too in Asia. Some of the best food.

"Why we chose Singapore at that time was it one of the most Westernized cities together with Hong Kong ready to accept these products. That's we started the first shops basically as sandwiches fresh and arranged in this city. We were quite sure this was the best place to go in because there was a ready-made demand.

"We started off in the downtown and later moved to residential areas, housing areas. Because people were very Westernized in the capital in their eating. Because we had a good product."

The first branch they opened was in the financial district.

Prince's tactic was to keep developing the concept, leading Delifrance into segments of the market where the competition was not as strong.

"It is a very competitive environment and you have got to be doing new things all the time. From the basic café at the beginning we went on to do a lot of activities. There were restaurants, the franchise of Fouchon; the 24 hour petrol station business, sidewalk cafes; a more upmarket café because we felt that the competition was coming on from the US and Starbucks and so on."

As competition came in the form of cafés, he positioned Delifrance in a different way because nobody French gave them any competition – and they were a bakery too. And with this type of bakery there was no sizeable competition.

"Then we developed some restaurants. And we brought over the company De La Notre in the middle so we had the capacity to start a restaurant. Then we developed the franchise for Fouchon with a restaurant and a café. Fouchon is quite renowned for its deli goods, luxury items, chocolates, pastries. They had shops and restaurants so they asked us to develop the business in Singapore. We developed one bakery for them and one café-restaurant.

"Once the concept was unveiled and well accepted, we knew we had a winning product. Once one niche of the product – the café-bakery – was a success we wanted to offer to the customer more and more possibilities to buy the same product in different forms in Singapore."

Delifrance moved into frozen products on the supermarket shelves and fresh products for the supermarket counter. They went into gas stations that are open 24 hours. They made sure standards of operations were very high. And made sure the retailers had the standards of quality under control as well.

"We started out in Singapore first. It took a lot of time, because we had to set up a factory first and it took us three years to break even. And once we started to break even, then we started country by country. We didn't move on to the third country until a second country was profitable and so on. It works because in term profitability and of control operations it helps.

"Outside of the café we used to sell in other ways – wholesale business. We developed some mini concepts with Esso gas stations were we had a takeaway counter. We did counter with baguettes, croissants, a few pastries inside the mini-market."

The wholesale division had over 300 wholesale customers, hotels, restaurants, supermarkets, clubs and airlines in Singapore.

Café-bakeries were specially designed to recreate the warmth and welcoming ambience of a Parisian café. "Le Bistrot" restaurants, as in France, a cosy and casual restaurant serving French home style dishes. Café-terrasse outlets using the Parisian sidewalk café concept. Take-aways located in supermarkets, department stores, and service stations. Delifrance also entered into a licensing arrangement with Esso to set up Delifrance bake-off corners in service stations; a French café-patisserie under the upmarket brand name "Fauchon," serving a wide range of high-end French foods and pastries.

Regional expansion

In 1987, Delifrance Asia began to actively pursue a strategy of regionalization of its operations which soon expanded into Hong Kong and the PRC (Peoples' Republic of China). The Group set up its own sales team in each country of operation to market its products.

With the expansion into regional markets, a restructuring exercise took place in 1989. Delifrance Asia became a management and investment holding company by transferring its operations in Singapore to a newly incorporated company, Delifrance Singapore.

The company intensified its efforts to expand its operations regionally in 1990, moving into Australia and Malaysia, first in the retail sector, followed by wholesale and manufacturing activities in each of the countries.

Eventually, Delifrance Asia had operations in Singapore, Malaysia, Hong Kong, the PRC, the Philippines, and Australia.

The Group and its joint venture companies operated 96 retail outlets and five factories employing approximately 1800 employees. In addition, they put franchising arrangements in place for the operation of 11 retail outlets and licensing arrangements for the operation of 16 bakery corners.

Expansion

Delifrance Hong Kong, a wholly-owned subsidiary, operates a factory to supply French bakery and pastry products to its retail outlets and for wholesale distribution, major hotels, restaurants, supermarkets, and private clubs in Hong Kong. Delifrance Hong Kong operates 16 retail outlets comprising café-bakeries which are located in carefully selected sites in key commercial and office districts in Hong Kong. In addition, Delifrance Hong Kong operates a bake-off counter which is situated in a business district.

In Australia, Delifrance established an extensive distribution network spanning most states in Australia for the distribution of frozen breads and viennoiseries. It has also employed its sales agents in most states. In addition, to improve its distribution capability in Sydney, it has its own fleet of refrigerated trucks to facilitate distribution.

In the PRC, Delifrance went into a joint venture. Vie de France Beijing was established in December 1986 as a 50%-owned joint venture company of Delifrance Asia with CITIC and FIRI. They set up a factory in Beijing for the manufacture and sale of French bakery and pastry products. The products are freshly baked in the factory and delivered to customers.

In 1991, Vie de France Beijing commenced the operation of retail outlets and production of frozen dough to supply to its own retail outlets. The first café-bakery was opened in Tiananmen Square in 1991 followed by five other café-bakeries and three bake-off/take-away corners in Beijing. Vie de France Beijing expects to open several other retail outlets in the near future to be financed from internal cash resources. The wholesale business accounts for a larger share of the turnover and profits of Vie de France Beijing as compared to its retail business. Its wholesale customers comprise mostly local shops and emporiums.

The IPO (1996)

"One year before everybody had postponed their IPO. But we decided to go to the market anyhow. We were very confident because at that time Delifrance was a company with a good track record, on turnover, profitability, and productivity. It was a focused company with a good management team at that time. It was a home-grown Singaporian company, with a good potential for growth. Everybody knew Delifrance.

"We didn't do any placement of shares. We went straight to the market. We wanted the customers of our shop to be our shareholders at the same time. We priced relatively high, because we were quite comfortable that a food company with a quality of focus and development was an attractive IPO."

The IPO offering, 45.2 million shares at 78 cents per share, was five and a half times oversubscribed. Shares closed at 97 cents on the first day of trading, a premium of 24% over the offer price. This was regarded as quite remarkable given the lackluster market conditions.

"It was a successful IPO," says Prince. "It showed that there was confidence in a home grown, quality company. And the press said because of our IPO, the market went up again – people went back to doing IPOs again a little bit."

"It wasn't really done to cash out. We went to the market because it was a long-term dream for the chairman of Vilgrain and because it was important for us in the management team. We were not keen to do it too soon because it would change things in the company. But you have to go when your trends are very good, when you have good growth. And when you can sell the dream to shareholders. You cannot go too late to the stock exchange."

The opportunity to exit came a year after the flotation, when the Vilgrain group decided to sell their share of the business to Semba Corporation, a Singapore-based conglomerate, in which government investment arms held a large stake.

Alexandre Vilgrain sold 2% of his 20.8% stake while Hugues Prince reduced his stake from 4.2% to 2.5%. They both undertook not to sell their remaining shares for ten years.

The financial press at the time expressed reservations about the price paid. SembCorp offered to purchase 51% of Delifrance Asia for $165.8 million in cash or $1.80 per share, valuing the company at more than 33 times earnings. The move was seen as part of Semb-Corp's diversification into "lifestyle" businesses, a strategy intended to reduce its reliance on its traditional marine engineering and shipping business, a sector which was suffering from the difficult economic conditions.

MILESTONES

» **1983**: GMP Foods Singapore Pte Ltd. starts to manufacture and distribute French bakery and pastry products under the trademark "Delifrance."

» **1987**: Company changes its name to Delifrance Asia Pte Ltd.

» **1989**: The Vilgrain family ceases to have any interest in Grands Moulins de Paris.

» **1989**: Delifrance Asia becomes a management and investment holding company, transferring its operations in Singapore to a newly incorporated company, Delifrance Singapore.

» **1990**: Opening of the first retail outlet in Sydney; first retail outlet was opened in Kuala Lumpur.

» **1995**: A joint venture was established in the Philippines for the manufacture and distribution of Delifrance products. In addition, a franchise agreement was signed for the operation of retail outlets in the Philippines.

» **1995**: Awarded the BHQ status by the Economic Development; helps Delifrance Asia to strengthen its operations in Singapore and in the region, as well as to develop its franchising activities in the region.

» **1996**: The Company was converted into a public limited company and adopted its present name Delifrance Asia Limited

» **1992–1997**: Delifrance Asia achieves a CAGR in turnover and earnings of 26% and 42% respectively.

» **1997**: IPO offering of 45.2 million shares at 78 cents per share was five and a half times oversubscribed.

» **1997**: SembCorp announces it has entered into an option agreement with Alexandre Vilgrain to purchase 51% of Delifrance Asia for $165.8mn in cash or $1.80 per share.
» **1998**: Alexander Vilgrain's departs as Chairman to make way for Chan Wing Leong, SembCorp's CFO.
» **1998**: Delifrance Asia acquired by Prudential Asset Management Asia Limited (PAMA), one of the largest private equity investment firms in Asia.

DIXONS' STAKE IN FREESERVE

Enterprise: Freeserve
Investor: Dixons Electrical
Exit strategy: Partial flotation, followed by trade sale
Payback: For a stake of £0.25mn in 1998, Dixons gained £120mn in cash on the flotation of Freeserve in 2000 and shares in Wanadoo, the French Internet service provider, worth £739mn.

Dixons and technology have, for better and worse, indelibly changed British lifestyle. The UK's leading computer and electrical retailer started life in a small photographic studio in Southend. Sixty-four years later Freeserve, their free Internet service operation, signed up its two millionth subscriber.

In between, Dixons had rarely ventured into uncharted territory, despite consistently delivering the latest user-friendly technology into the homes, hands, and hearts of an increasingly expectant British public. However, the ultimate end of the Freeserve chapter could well depend upon the salutary lessons learned from one occasion that it did.

Dixons' first foray into a new technology venture is probably best forgotten. In 1987, they acquired Silo, which was then the third largest electrical retailer in the USA. The market was fragmented; Silo had only 147 stores, so the logic for consolidation appeared sound.

Unfortunately Dixons bought near the 1987 peak, and Silo became a money pit – Dixons seemed to be following that very British tradition of losing its shirt in America. They eventually disposed of their US interests to Fretter Inc. in 1993, but the exit was not complete, as Dixons was obliged to retain a 30% interest in Fretter.

This unhappy chapter only closed in 1996 when the investment was finally written off. 1996 was a watershed year for Dixons in other ways, too: Stanley Kalms, their founder and chairman, was knighted for his services to electrical retailing in the UK and Dixons regained its position in the FTSE 100.

It was three years earlier, however, that a 29-year-old John Pluthero, with a background in finance, consulting, and strategy, joined Dixons from Coopers & Lybrand. Having undertaken a number of planning, strategic, and operational roles he became Dixons' corporate development director. In formulating the group's Internet strategy he has been largely credited with devising, developing, and launching Freeserve for what is now the bargain basement price of £240,000 – unequivocally the greatest ever short-term investment in Sir Stanley's long and celebrated career.

How Kalms collected!

On the September 22, 1998, Dixons group chief executive, John Clare, announced the launch of Freeserve. He described it as "the UK's first fully featured Internet service that is available free, with no registration or subscription fees and no hourly online charges."

"From tomorrow morning," Clare announced, " you can walk into Dixons, Curry's, PC World or The Link, pick up a free CD, load the software and you're ready to go with unlimited free Internet use. All the Freeserve customer pays is their normal charge for a local rate telephone call."

At the time Freeserve went live there was already a small number of subscription-free ISPs (Internet service providers) in operation, such as X-Stream and ConnectFree, but they went largely unnoticed as the Freeserve CDs went like hotcakes.

Within five months Freeserve had opened one million customer accounts and had knocked AOL off the top spot to become market leader. Half the customers were new to the Internet: Freeserve was not for the anoraks or geeks; Freeserve was for the great British public.

On the June 7, 1999, when Dixons announced it was to float a minority stake in Freeserve, customer accounts had grown to one and a half million and development was gathering tremendous pace. The decision to float was made following a review undertaken by the company's advisers, Credit Suisse First Boston and Cazenove. Sir Stanley said "Freeserve will have greater flexibility in pursuing its strategy in the rapidly growing and evolving Internet sector."

Which possibly translated into: "With the real prospects of any profits a very long way off and an insatiable appetite for more and more investment, this venture could be extremely detrimental to our core business unless we use somebody else's money to invest with."

On August 2, after only ten months in operation, Freeserve was listed on the LSE and NASDAQ, with Dixons continuing to own 79% of the shares.

The offering was 30 times subscribed. It was the largest Internet flotation at that time. At the offer price of £1.50 a share Freeserve was valued at a remarkable £1.51bn.

Remarkable indeed, as in just over seven months trading to May 1, 1999 it incurred a net loss of £1.04mn on revenues of £2.73mn.

Tiger by the tail!

The share price started on its very own roller-coaster ride. Having made dramatic opening gains, the shares dropped to a low of £1.34 on October 28.

Then in November the roller-coaster moved into top gear. In December the shares hit nearly £6.00. In January they broke through £8.00 and in February they broke through £9.00. Freeserve's value was now greater than its astounded and infinitely elder parent.

In March, after only 18 months in business, Freeserve joined the FTSE 100. By this time Sir Stanley must have felt that he had fallen off his much-walked tightrope and was now in the circus ring holding an extremely large tiger by an extremely short tail.

Even before it joined the FTSE, Freeserve shares started to free-fall as the Internet rush abated. At the beginning of March the shares fell to £6.00, by the end of March, £5.00 and in April £3.80. By the end of April, however, they started to rise again on the back of rumors of an imminent £6.00 a share offer from Germany's T-Online.

On May 8, in response to this speculation, Dixons publicly confirmed it was considering its options in respect of its shareholding in Freeserve and that since then discussions had been held with a number of parties including T-Online. Whilst certain discussions continued, it was not expected that "this process would lead in the near future to a bid for the whole of Freeserve."

The shares moved down slightly but then shot back up to around £5.40 in late May. £5.40 proved to be the dead cat bounce. The tiger had expired!

A global tsunami of dotcom sentiment had swept through the markets and – combined with the stark realization that there were up to 500 other wannabe ISPs out there at various stages of development – the share price plummeted. On October 23, Freeserve dropped out of the FTSE 100 with a share price of £1.63.

By the time Wanadoo, the French ISP, made its all share bid for Freeserve in early December, its offer valued each share at approximately £1.57.

This was more than a 10% premium on the closing Freeserve share price of the previous day. The deal was completed on February 16, 2001, with Dixons exchanging its 79% holding in Freeserve for a 12.7% share in Wanadoo.

Wanadoo's own freefall had started in September 2000. With its shares at 22 Euros, they fell to just above 12 as the bid rumors started, fell to 11 when the offer was made and fell to near 5 towards the end of March before gradually rising to 7 at the end of May.

On the May 4, John Clare said "The development and sale of Freeserve added substantial value to the Group. Dixons invested a total of £240,000 in Freeserve. The Group received £120mn in cash on the flotation of Freeserve and its stake in Wanadoo is currently worth £739mn."[3]

He went on to say "Much credit for these achievements must go to the commitment and enthusiasm of all of our staff. By way of a 'thank you' this bonus share plan recognizes and rewards our employees for their contribution to this success."

Freeserve was an unequivocally brilliant venture, but it wasn't risk-free. It was a very definite departure from Dixons' core competencies. Prising the initial £240,000 from the company coffers, for a radical departure from the mainstream business, would have been a non-starter in many organizations. It could have resulted in an indeterminable cost overrun at the very least, while losing it all was a distinct possibility and would have caused considerable embarrassment. The costs of the IPO (reportedly £12.1mn) would have to have been absorbed somewhere had the issue failed.

The heavy ongoing investment in further developing the Freeserve offering could have had major repercussions on Dixons' core operations before a penny of profit was seen. Before the Freeserve chapter of the Dixons story closes, however, Sir Stanley can be acclaimed as being one of the very few who collected real rewards out of the virtual reality of the Internet boom.

Exiting the story

Wanadoo's shares stand at €3.81.[4] Dixons is the second largest shareholder after France Telecom. Wanadoo's interim results for 2001 showed net losses rising to €102mn Euros from €67mn last time. Sir Stanley "retires" after 55 years in 2002, becoming President of Dixons.

Dixons can unwind its Wanadoo shareholding, but said at the time of the deal that it was planning to maintain long-term holdings. The world markets are in turmoil. So how and when will this chapter end?

DIXONS: THE FIRST 60 YEARS

- » **1937**: Dixons Studio Limited incorporated.
- » **1939–45**: Portrait photography flourishes during the War years and business grows to seven studios.
- » **1950s**: Extensive advertising, customer credit, and mail order success makes Dixons the leading photographic dealer in the UK.
- » **1962**: Dixons launched on the London Stock Exchange.
- » **1980s**: Dixons launches own-brand audio, TV, and video products, acquires Currys Supasnaps and Silo.
- » **1993**: Silo and Supasnaps sold.

FREESERVE TIMELINE

- » **1996**: Wanadoo created as the Internet access service of France Telecom.

> » **1998 (September)**: Freeserve launched by Dixons.
> » **1999 (August)**: Freeserve partially floated on London Stock Exchange/NASDAQ.
> » **2000 (March)**: Freeserve enters FTSE 100.
> » **2000 (July)**: Wanadoo partially floated on Paris Premier Marché.
> » **2000 (December)**: Wanadoo bids for Freeserve.
> » **2001 (February)**: Wanadoo/Freeserve deal completed.

NOTES

1 This section was compiled with reference to the following: Cassy, John (2000) "ARM acts to break mobile dependency." *The Guardian*, March 12; Unattributed (2000) "Interview with Robin Saxby." *Enterprise*, May/June; and personal interviews by the author (2001) with Herman Hauser (September 27), Will Schmidt (September 26), and Larry Tesler (October 3).

2 This section was compiled with reference to the following: Delifrance Asia Ltd listing document 1996; *The Business Times*, Singapore, October 8, 1996; Analyst reports (http://www.geocities.com/Wall Street/1257/deli.html); author's personal interviews with Hugues Prince, August/September 2001.

3 Based on a May 3, 2001 price of €6.7 and an exchange rate of €1.61 to £1 sterling.

4 As at September 21, 2001.

Key Concepts and Thinkers

» An A–Z glossary of the topic.
» Brief details of some of the key thinkers on exit strategies.

PAUL A. BUTLER

Paul A. Butler, the McKinsey consultant, highlights some of the misconceptions about LBO firms. Managers in companies where an LBO of an underperforming division has taken place often console themselves, says Butler, with a combination of false beliefs; namely that the new owners:

» are looking to transfer their companies to a greater fool in the shortest possible time;
» are financial magicians who turn solid balance sheets into smoke and mirrors; and
» recklessly slash and burn sound businesses in their selfish quest for quick returns.

On the contrary, says Butler. Far from ripping companies apart for a quick buck, LBO firms' need to generate higher cash flows from operations and repay high levels of debt compels them to improve the performance of their companies. Freed from the constraints of the corporate center, LBO firms can more easily make difficult decisions about cutting jobs and disposing of businesses, removing unnecessary costs and improving capital productivity.

Butler bases his findings on the results of financial analyses of many deals in the chemicals sector, as well as interviews with dozens of people experienced in buying, selling, and operating leveraged chemicals buy-outs, (see *McKinsey Quarterly*, 2001, number 2).

Traditional chemicals companies, says Butler, have to compete against these new players that focus relentlessly on performance and growth. And this is no short-term trend. The amount of new funds seeking investment and the huge restructuring opportunities created by the disintegration of European chemicals conglomerates (especially in France and Germany) point to more, not less, LBO activity.

Chemicals companies must therefore take action, he says, since every one of them includes businesses that sit uncomfortably in the portfolio, dragging down share prices and putting them within reach of predators. Such companies have four options.

1. Get the best deal from financial buyers

Traditional chemicals corporations don't always get the best possible deal when they sell their businesses to LBO firms. In 1998, for example, Hoechst sold its Vianova Resins business to Morgan Grenfell Private Equity for $542mn. Only 12 months later, Morgan Grenfell resold Vianova to Solutia in a trade sale worth $640mn – an almost instant profit of nearly 20%.

Financial buyers pay less on average not only because of their dispassionate approach to acquisitions but also because they tend to negotiate downward during the due-diligence phase from a price that had earlier been accepted in principle. Once LBO firms find themselves the sole bidder, they are skilled at discovering problems (for instance, environmental liabilities or outdated equipment) in the seller's business offer.

Chemicals companies can respond in a number of ways. They should maintain a competitive auction right up to the last minute, because so many LBO firms, not to mention trade buyers, are interested in chemicals acquisitions. To boost the buyer's confidence in the senior managers of the business to be sold, the seller should also involve them in the negotiations. And if the selling company maintains a small equity stake in the business – say, 10 or 20%, possibly with a seat on the board – it will have a chance to learn how LBO firms achieve their high levels of return.

Selling non-core businesses to financial buyers is a low-risk approach and, in many cases, one that is preferable to hanging on to under-performing assets indefinitely. Fortunately, the LBO market is now sufficiently competitive that any business, except for one with massive environmental liabilities, should be able to fetch a fair price.

2. Execute an internal LBO

The second option, an internal LBO, aims to create as much value as LBO houses might, but to capture the gain for a company's own shareholders. This course sounds simple, but its rarity in the chemicals industry, and indeed in most others, should bear witness to its difficulty. An internal LBO has a better chance of succeeding if a corporation has nothing to lose – that is, if the business unit is small and non-core or can't be sold for a reasonable price.

Unfortunately, corporate centers find it hard to resist the temptation to interfere in the operation of anything they own. When business managers whose companies have made the transition from ownership by corporations to ownership by LBO firms give interviews, they always emphasize that independence from the corporate center is the most important factor for success.

There is a range of financial structures, ranging from an internal carve-out to a joint venture with a private investment firm, that could be applied to an internal LBO. Their common features include high leverage, equity purchased with personal funds by the senior-management team, and complete operational and strategic freedom for those managers. The other important feature is the possibility of exit routes similar to those that might be expected in a real LBO. There can be no guarantee for the equity stakes of managers, but they must be able to have a reasonable expectation that, in the absence of an IPO, the parent might reacquire the business or that it could be sold to a trade buyer or re-capitalized.

3. Undertake a leveraged re-capitalization

The third alternative, a leveraged re-capitalization of an entire company, is riskier than an internal LBO because the former makes the entire company more highly leveraged. Unlike a company that goes private, a re-capitalized company retains its public shareholders, has stock quoted on a public exchange, and publishes the usual financial data. The difference is that more of the equity is placed in the hands of senior management, and possibly other employees, thus strengthening the incentive to maximize the company's performance.

Union Carbide conducted a leveraged re-capitalization in 1985. Saddled with the consequences of a disastrous diversification and a serious accident at an Indian pesticide plant, the company faced a hostile bid from GAF, a much smaller player. Carbide saved itself from GAF's attentions by going into debt to repurchase 55% of its shares at a price GAF couldn't match. It then sold off its battery unit – which included Ever Ready Batteries, one of Carbide's best-performing businesses – and used the proceeds to pay off the debt. This defensive re-capitalization forced Carbide to focus on just a few sectors of the petrochemicals industry, a strategy that was successful for nearly 15 years.

4. Take the whole company private

The approach that goes about as far as possible on the risk-and-reward spectrum is to take the whole company private in a leveraged management buy-out (MOB). Although the returns might prove spectacular, much personal wealth would have to be ventured, so it isn't surprising that the chemicals industry provides few examples. One of them was the buy-out of most of the equity in GAF by Sam Heyman in 1989 and its flotation two years later.

That deal took place more than ten years ago. Today's executives must avoid accusations that a management buy-out would permit a few insiders to make huge gains at the expense of thousands of public shareholders. To put the problem another way, no deal that shareholders would find acceptable is likely to give MBO participants the returns they desire.

Yet in some parts of the economy, management buy-outs of whole companies have become quite fashionable. In UK commercial property, for example, a rash of participants – including MEPC, the sector's fourth-largest player – went private last year. More and more people think that market quotations for property companies have outlived their usefulness, since buying a group of assets and collecting rents can never deliver equity-like rates of return on investment.

The chemicals industry as a whole hasn't reached that stage in its evolution yet, though some of its sectors, such as European fibers and fertilizers, are perilously close.

Chemicals companies should take advantage of the LBO firms' current appetite for their businesses and sell more unwanted assets. The present state of affairs probably won't last indefinitely, since LBO firms are likely to find it increasingly hard to exit from chemicals deals.

The IPO route is closed for the foreseeable future, and trade sales are becoming more difficult because regulators fear that acquirers may raise their market concentration to unacceptable levels. As an alternative, companies could try the LBO approach to creating value; they might find that as much as 50% of their business could benefit, which would imply a huge overall improvement in their performance.

KAPLAN AND STRÖMBERG[1]

Kaplan and Strömberg are interested in how venture capital specialists appraise potential investments. They studied investments made by 10 venture capital firms in 42 portfolio companies in the late 1990s, using the analyses the VCs produced at the time. They also looked at the financial contracts for the investments to see how VCs' appraisals relate to contractual terms and subsequent performance.

At the time of their analysis, 18 (43%) of the companies in their sample remained private; 10 firms (24%) had gone public; 3 (7%) had been sold and 1 (2%) had been liquidated. Of course it is possible that some of those that were still private would ultimately be successful, particularly as one-half of the investments in the sample had been made in the three years prior to the analysis.

Like most academic and anecdotal accounts, they found that VCs consider explicitly the attractiveness of the opportunity, the management team, and the deal terms. In at least half of the investments, the VCs expected to play an important role in recruiting management.

Their study confirms that the VC's initial appraisal of the management team is particularly important. Their key finding is that stronger management teams obtain more attractive contracts and are more likely to take their companies public.

Portfolio companies with management teams perceived to be strong are almost three times more likely to have gone public than companies with management teams perceived to be neutral or weak. On the other hand, there is no difference in IPO likelihood for firms with markets perceived to be attractive from those perceived to be neutral.

This supports the views of some VCs that management is the most important ingredient in evaluating an investment.

They were surprised by their results concerning the effect of competition on subsequent outcome. Companies with weak competition receive less attractive contracts and are less likely to go public. Only 6% of the companies with weak perceived competition at the time of the investment had gone public, compared to 38% of the companies with strong or some competition. They find this result counterintuitive, but the commonsense view is that any market worth operating in will have competition.

The results also indicate that firms with strategies perceived as risky are less likely to have gone public, at 5% and 11% respectively, than the typical firm in the sample.

Taken together, the results indicate a strong emphasis and importance on the appraisal of the management teams. Strong management teams obtain more attractive contracts and perform better – at least as measured by the likelihood of going public.

JOSHUA LERNER[2]

Joshua Lerner, professor at Harvard Business School, has studied the effects of distribution policies on the returns that venture capitalists make to their partners when investment funds mature.

Lerner concludes that venture capitalists have an incentive to time the distribution of fund proceeds to maximize their own compensation and the apparent value of returns from the fund. This is the most important marketing tool when it comes to raising money for a new fund. They could use their inside knowledge of their portfolio firms, he suggests, to work out when the share price has peaked, timing the distribution accordingly.

Venture capital funds are organized as limited partnerships. The venture capitalist serves as the general partner and the other investors as limited partners – individuals, corporations, and pension funds.

VCs realize their stakes in portfolio companies that have gone public, in two ways. They can sell their shares in the market and distribute the cash to the limited partners. More often, however, they distribute the actual shares to each of the limited partners, keeping their share of the proceeds based on the value of the stock on the day the distribution is declared.

Increasingly, venture capitalists have moved to stock distribution as a way of distributing the proceeds from their investment funds. There are often tax advantages for partners in receiving shares rather than cash; and government regulations generally restrict the size of sales by corporate insiders, the officers and directors of the firm and anybody who owns more than 10% of the shares equity.

But, says Lerner, if the shares are overvalued, the VC has an incentive to distribute shares, rather than cash. The VC's track record is its most important asset, when it comes to raising money for a new fund.

Returns for the venture capital fund are calculated on basis of the closing price of the stock on the day of distribution. If the market reacts to the distribution by marking down the value of the shares, the calculated return will be higher that the actual price limited partners achieve, as they don't actually receive their shares for a day or two after the distribution is declared.

Similarly, according to Lerner, VCs have an incentive to distribute shares, in order to maximize their own compensation. At payback time, the VC distributes the proceeds in proportion to the capital contribution that each investor has contributed, hanging on to their own share (typically the venture capitalist contributes 1% of the fund's capital). Once committed capital has been returned, the VC hangs on to a much larger share of the profits, typically 20%. Distributing overvalued shares moves the fund more quickly to the point where the VC starts receiving profits.

GLOSSARY

Acquisition – Any deal where the bidder ends up with 50% or more of the target is called an acquisition. A bidder is the entity that makes the purchase or the offer to purchase. The target is the entity being purchased, or the entity in which a stake is being purchased. The vendor is the entity that sells or disposes of the target entity.

BIMBO – A combination of management buy-out and buy-in where the team buying the business includes both existing management and new managers.

Bond – The generic name for a tradeable loan security issued by governments and companies as a means of raising capital. Government bonds are known as gilts or Treasury Stock.

Debt – This may include bank loans, overdrafts, and lease financing and may be long- or short-term, secured or unsecured. The lender receives interest at an agreed rate and in the event that this is not paid may be entitled to take control of and sell certain assets owned by the company. A lender does not, however, generally have a share in the ownership of the business.

Development capital – Also known as expansion capital. This is venture capital financing used for expansion of an already established company.

Due diligence – This is one of the main processes that takes place before a transaction (e.g. MBO/MBI) is completed. The aim is to ensure that there is nothing that contradicts the financier's understanding of the current state and potential of the business. The individual elements of due diligence may include commercial due diligence (markets, product, and customers), a market report (marketing study), an accountant's report (trading record, net asset and taxation position) and legal due diligence (implications of litigation, title to assets, and intellectual property issues).

BIT – Earnings before interest and tax.

EBITDA – Earnings before interest, tax, depreciation, and amortization. EBITDA is measure of cash flow. By excluding interest, taxes, depreciation, and amortization, the amount of money a company is bringing in can be clearly seen.

Equity – The term used to describe shares in a business conveying ownership of that business. The shareholders may be entitled to dividends. If a business fails, the shareholders will only receive a distribution on winding up after the lenders and creditors have been paid. An equity investment, therefore, has a higher risk attached to it than that facing a bank lender and thus the return that the shareholders demand on their money is typically higher. The most common source of equity finance for buy-outs is the venture capital market.

Exit (realization) – The point at which the institutional investors realize their investment. Venture capitalists may, depending on the business and their own situation, look to achieve an exit in anything from a few months to 10 years. Exits generally occur via trade sales, secondary management buy-outs and flotation on the stock market, or by write-off if the investment ends in receivership.

Goodwill – The difference between the price that is paid for a business and the value of its assets.

High-yield (junk) bonds – Bonds that offer high rates of interest but with correspondingly higher risk attached to the capital.

IBO (institutional buy-out) – This is when a private equity house acquires a business directly from the vendor. Often the target's management will take a small stake.

IPO (initial public offering) – Shares in a company have been placed on a stock exchange. An IPO is always just the first time a company's shares are listed – if a company has a listing on another market or in another country, then the listing is not an IPO, merely a secondary, or additional, listing.

IRR (internal rate of return) – The average annual compound rate of return received by an investor over the life of their investment. This is a key indicator used by institutions in appraising their investments.

Joint venture – Two or more companies that form a new venture.

Liquidity – The availability of a currency used to trade in a particular market e.g. ability to trade in and out of shares in high volume without a significant impact on their price.

LBU (leveraged build-up) – A venture capital firm builds up the company it owns by acquiring smaller companies to amalgamate into the larger firm, thus increasing the total value of its investments through synergies between the acquired companies.

LBO (leveraged buy-out) – Takeover of a company by investors who use the company's own assets as collateral to raise the money which finances the bid. Normally the loans are then repaid from the company's cash flow, or by selling some of its assets. Term used mainly in North America.

Management buy-outs (MBOs) and management buy-ins (MBIs) – Allow entrepreneurial management teams to buy divisions of larger companies thus unleashing new entrepreneurial skills, improving the results of often underperforming businesses and creating smaller, more flexible enterprises.

The MBO and MBI are recognized as successful mechanisms for revitalizing companies and generating strong shareholder returns. They are popular across all sectors of industry because they allow managers considerable personal reward in return for assuming ownership and responsibility for their businesses whilst providing private equity funds with good returns.

MBI (management buy-in) – Purchase of the business or business unit by a new team of managers, with the new management team taking a majority stake. This often happens with family firms who have no one to pass the company on to, so they sell the company to a management team. The old owners sometimes retain a small stake.

The management team often includes a venture capital firm. If the venture capital firm take a majority stake then the deal is classed as an IBO (institutional buy-in), rather than an MBI.

MBO (management buy-out) – This is the purchase of a business by its management, usually in co-operation with outside financiers. Buy-outs vary in size, scope, and complexity but the key feature is that the managers acquire an equity interest in their business, sometimes a controlling stake, for a relatively modest personal investment. The existing owners sell most or usually all of their investment to the managers and their co-investors. If the outside financier (e.g. venture capital firm) takes a majority stake then the deal is not an MBO but an IBO (institutional buy-out).

Merger – A true merger is actually quite rare. Many acquisitions are described as mergers but in a true merger, there is a one-for-one share swap, for shares in the new company. If the swap is not on equal terms then this is an acquisition.

Mezzanine finance – This is often used to bridge the gap between the secured debt a business can support, the available equity, and the purchase price. Because of this, and because it normally ranks behind senior debt in priority of repayment, unsecured mezzanine debt commands a significantly higher rate of return than senior debt and often carries warrants (options to buy ordinary shares) to subscribe for ordinary shares. It ranks behind more formal borrowing contracts and is thus referred to as "subordinated" or "intermediate debt."

Ordinary shares – Ordinary shareholders carry full rights to participate in the business through voting in general meetings. They are entitled to payment of a dividend out of profits and ultimately repayment of capital in the event of liquidation, but only after other claims have been met. As owners of the company the ordinary shareholders bear the greatest risk, but also enjoy the fruits of corporate success in the form of higher dividends and/or capital gains.

Preference shares – These fall between debt and equity. They usually carry no voting rights and have preferential rights over ordinary shareholders regarding dividends and ultimate repayment of capital in the event of liquidation.

Private equity – Private equity provides equity capital to enterprises not quoted on a stock market. Private equity can be used to develop new products and technologies, to expand working capital, to make acquisitions, or to strengthen a company's balance sheet. It can also resolve ownership and management issues – a succession in family-owned companies, or the buy-out or buy-in of a business by experienced managers may be achieved using private equity.

Private equity is an increasingly widely used term in Europe and is generally interchangeable with venture capital, but some commentators use it to refer only to the management buy-out and buy-in investment sector.

Privatization – A government, council or other state-owned entity disposes of a company or stake in a company that it owns. The company, or part of the company, moves from public to private ownership.

Public to private buy-out – This involves the management or a private equity provider making an offer for the shares of a publicly quoted company, then taking the company private.

Ratchet – A mechanism whereby management's equity stake may be increased (or decreased) on the occurrence of various future events, typically when the institutional investor's returns exceed a particular target rate.

Reverse takeover – An unlisted company acquires a smaller listed company, thus achieving a stock market listing "through the back door." The acquisition is carried out by the listed company issuing new shares in order to acquire the unlisted company. As the unlisted company is larger than the listed one, the bidder has to issue so many new shares that the owners of the unlisted company end up with a controlling stake in the listed company.

Secondary buy-out – The management team in conjunction with a private equity funder, acquires the business, allowing the existing private equity supplier to exit from its investment.

Second-round financing – Most companies need more than the initial injection of capital, whether to enable them to expand into new markets, develop more production capacity, or to overcome temporary problems. There can be several rounds of financing.

Senior debt – Debt provided by a bank, usually secured and ranking ahead of other loans and borrowings in the event of a winding up.

Shares – Certificates or book entries representing ownership in a business.

Start-up capital – Capital used to establish a company from scratch or within the first few months of its existence. Risky but with huge potential returns for the very successful.

Syndicated investment – Where an investment is too large, complex or risky, the lead investor may seek other financiers to share the investment. This process is known as syndication.

Trade sale – The commonest method of exit is a sale to a trade buyer. This can either allow management to withdraw from the business, or it may open up the prospect of working in a larger enterprise.

Vendor finance – Can either be in the form of deferred loans from, or shares subscribed by, the vendor. The vendor may well take shares alongside the management in the new entity. This category of finance is generally used where the vendor's expectation of the value of the business is higher than that of management and the institutions backing them.

Venture capital – Equity finance invested in an unquoted, and usually quite young, company to enable it to start up, expand or restructure its operations entirely. Early stage i.e. seed and start-up and expansion finance is cheaper than bank finance, initially, because paying dividends can be deferred; but it implies handing over some control to the financial backer, together with a share of earnings and decisions over future sales.

There are variations in what is meant by venture capital and private equity in different countries. Venture capital is, strictly speaking, a subset of private equity and refers to equity investments made for the launch, early development, or expansion of a business. In Europe, these terms are generally used interchangeably and venture capital includes management buy-outs and buy-ins (MBO/MBIs). This is in contrast to the US, where MBO/MBIs are not classified as venture capital.

NOTES

1 See "How Do Venture Capitalists Choose Investments?" Steven N. Kaplan and Per Strömberg, August 2000.

2 See "A note on distributions of venture investments." Prof. Joshua Lerner, Harvard Business School, January 1995.

Resources

- » Books and general information.
- » Venture capital companies and associations.
- » Research and academic institutions.

This chapter provides a brief summary of seminal articles, books, practitioners, useful Websites, etc. that you may find useful for further research into exit strategies and venture capital.

BOOKS AND GENERAL INFORMATION

Bygrave, W.D., Hay, M. & Peters, J.B. *The Venture Capital Handbook*. Financial Times/Prentice Hall, London.

Birley, S. & Muzyka, D. (eds.) (1997) *Mastering Enterprise*. Financial Times/Prentice Hall, London.

Gompers, P. & Lerner, J. (1999) *The Venture Capital Cycle*. MIT Press, Boston.

Rickertsen, R., with Gunther, R. (2001) *Buyout*, American Management Association, New York.

Other published information
Asset Alternatives
This specialist information provider on the private equity marketplace has operated since 1991. The firm publishes newsletters, directories, and research reports and runs conferences. The *Corporate Venturing Report* is Asset Alternatives' flagship newsletter. It also publishes *The Corporate Venturing Directory and Yearbook*.

Both are available from Asset Alternatives, 170 Linden Street, Wellesley, MA 02482. (Fax +1 781 304 1540. Tel +1 781 304 1500)

PricewaterhouseCoopers MoneyTree Survey
This is a survey conducted in partnership with VentureOne (see above), designed to take the cleanest measure of "core" investments in venture-backed companies in the United States, providing meaningful statistics on the venture industry. Full details can be found at www.pwcmoneytree.com.

On-line resources
Frontier, *Business Week*'s resource for small business, can be found at www.businessweek.com.

Yahoo's small business information is at www.yahoo.com.

VENTURE CAPITAL COMPANIES AND ASSOCIATIONS

3I is a venture capital company that provides capital to enable growth for start-up companies, expanding businesses, buy-outs and buy-ins; sector expertise and industry contacts on a global scale. Its Website can be found at www.3i.com/worldwide.

Venture One's comprehensive database on venture backed companies and investors, events, and publications makes interesting reading: www.ventureone.com.

Initiative Europe is a UK-based risk capital specialist. Its Website can be found at www.initiativeeurope.com.

Venture economics

National Venture Capital Association

The National Venture Capital Association (NVCA) is a member-based trade association that represents the North American venture capital industry. Its Website is www.nvca.org.

European Private Equity and Venture Capital Association

This association was established in 1983 to represent, promote, and facilitate the development of the European private equity and venture capital industry. As the industry's pan-European representative body with 740 members, EVCA supports a wide range of initiatives designed to encourage an entrepreneurial environment in Europe, promote the industry to institutional investors worldwide, encourage the development of equity markets appropriate to the needs of private equity investors, and establish high standards of business conduct and professional competence. The association stimulates promotion, research, and analysis of private equity and facilitates contacts with policy-makers, investors, research institutions, universities, trade associations, and other relevant organizations. Its Website can be found at www.evca.com.

RESEARCH AND ACADEMIC INSTITUTIONS

Babson College

The Arthur M. Blank Center for Entrepreneurship at Babson College is a leading US center for research and teaching in entrepreneurial management. With LBS (see below) and more than 20 academic partners, it produces the Global Entrepreneurship Monitor.

INSEAD/3I Venturelab

A joint venture between the European business school and the venture capital specialist, this organization provides research and advice on entrepreneurial management. This includes reports on comparison between managers who remain in companies and those who join an MBO; factors that determine the climate for enterprise in European countries. The Website is found at www.insead.edu.

London Business School

This institution has a Foundation for Entrepreneurial Management; a world-renowned center for research, teaching, and practice of entrepreneurial management. Its Website is at www.lbs.edu.

The Center for Management Buy-out Research (COMBER)

COMBER was founded at Nottingham University Business School in March 1986 to monitor and analyze management buy-outs in a comprehensive and analytical way. As an independent body, COMBER has developed a wide-ranging and detailed database of almost 16,000 companies, which provides the only complete set of statistics on management buy-outs and buy-ins in Europe. COMBER publishes regular reports on buy-out trends and relevant issues in its *Quarterly Review* and annual *European Management Buy-out Review*.

Ten Steps to Making Exit Strategies Work

- » Exit strategies – have one!
- » Avoid the living dead.
- » Drive towards an IPO – adopt a default strategy.
- » Tell a good story.
- » But make the bottom line sing.
- » Focus on the fundamentals.
- » Don't confuse objectives.
- » Set expectations, then exceed them.
- » Widen the net.
- » Exit smiling.

1. EXIT STRATEGIES – HAVE ONE!

Exit planning is not a cure-all for every aspect of business performance. But the advantages of thinking about an exit, for example, more focused decision-making, will generally be of benefit to the day-to-day management of a company. The most important thing about exit strategies is to have one in the first place. It is vitally important for entrepreneurs and investors to have a shared view of the investment horizon and the way value is to be realized.

People won't follow you up a cul-de-sac, so make sure you have thought out, and discussed, the exit route you are aiming for before you start to do the deal.

2. AVOID THE LIVING DEAD

There's a word in the venture capital industry for companies stuck in your portfolio that nobody wants. They're called the living dead. Anyone that has any experience in venture capital, being on the board of a living dead company for nine years, realizes that you do deals that you want to sell. You're a hero if you do an IPO. You're an idiot if you're on the board for nine years and just get your money back. That's not a job for a dynamic entrepreneur.

3. DRIVE TOWARDS AN IPO – THE BEST DEFAULT STRATEGY

The exit that finally occurs may well turn out to be different than the one you planned or expected. Real life has a knack of overtaking plans and it is not smart to ignore new opportunities that come along unexpectedly.

The best companies, as our case studies in Chapter 7 show, generally exit through a combination of astute planning and the opportunism that characterizes the entrepreneurial approach to managing the business. But aiming at an IPO may well be the best default strategy. In Europe, IPOs form only 20–30% of the exits; most are trade sales.

Driving to an IPO is usually a good thing because it gives you an outsider's perspective and forces you to take on board the most important factors for success, the lessons of best practice. For example, that you require robust management, international accounting standards, and a solid management team. It's getting the business in shape whatever the outcome.

4. TELL A GOOD STORY

There's a sense of excitement about a successful flotation. A decent track record and cashflow are simply prerequisites for a successful IPO. It's the anticipation of high returns in the future that sparks the interest. Telling a good story in the lead-up to a flotation is an essential part of capturing the fancy of the public.

5. BUT MAKE THE BOTTOM LINE SING

It's a simple guiding principle, but one that some managers preparing a business for exit overlook, especially if they get caught up playing high finance. There are many ways to exit a business, but the best exit strategy is to build a high-quality business. There's only one way you can be sure to find someone interested in taking it on – it has to be worth buying. However buoyant the IPO market, however booming your industry sector, however keen a buyer is to spend their money, you won't benefit unless you have a strong company to sell.

The best time to sell is when things are going well. But even if markets are down, the stronger your position, the more you can pick and choose the timing of a disposal. Make the most of presenting the company in the best light, certainly, but put the effort into making the bottom line sing.

6. FOCUS ON THE FUNDAMENTALS

The bottom-line test says you shouldn't be investing at all unless you're aiming to make loads of money, preferably bucket-loads. Aim for less and the chances are that's all you'll achieve.

7. DON'T CONFUSE OBJECTIVES

Thinking about exit is the first step in aligning objectives between investor and the entrepreneurial management team. Don't mix them up. A corporate's objectives at exit can be very different: it all depends on what kind of a deal it is.

At one end of the spectrum there's an M&A deal, the corporate buying something they want. At the other end could be a minority venture investment in a company in whose technology they're interested. In between there's a direct investment in a company to cement some sort of rights: product rights for a biotech company; exclusive rights in your territory to market somebody's software; technology license rights for your core product. The objectives are very different. On one hand the corporate doesn't care what happens to the investee company; they just wants to make an outrageous financial gain. On the other hand they may want to acquire the company. Then in the middle, they may not want it but they don't want it to go to a competitor.

There used to be this feeling that strategic and financial objectives for a corporate were inversely correlated. You want the technology and the company to be outrageously successful. A corporate is going to want to invest in somebody that's successful in the marketplace.

8. SET EXPECTATIONS, THEN EXCEED THEM

How you set expectations about performance is a separate issue: under promise, over deliver works well for many.

9. WIDEN THE NET

Remember that competitors may be the likely purchasers: they will pay more for a business which can be merged to provide profit improvements. If they do not buy, their interest will increase the price.

10. EXIT SMILING

Whether you retire to spend more time with your money or move on to the next entrepreneurial challenge, if you've pulled off a successful exit, you can give yourself a pat on the back for the hard work you put in at the outset. Spot things for management to consider to enhance the business and make exit easier. Issues like:

» PR/Marketing: advertising and marketing do not just sell the product – they may help sell the business.
» Financial Statements: ensure they are consistent from year to year.

» Reporting systems requirements: should be addressed from Day 1.
» Legal structure: avoid minority stakes which do not have a strategic purpose or try to eliminate them prior to exit. Remember, one single shareholder can hold up the whole process.
» Make sure there's a management plan for succession.

Frequently Asked Questions (FAQs)

Q1: What is an exit strategy?

A: An exit strategy is the plan for how you will realize a return from your investment. See Chapter 1.

Q2: What are the most common methods of exiting from an investment in a business project?

A: Failed business aside, trade sales, flotations, and buy-outs are the three most common forms of exit. See Chapter 2 under *Exit routes*.

Q3: Where does the capital for a business project come from?

A: When a business is starting up, family, friends, working partners, and business angels are more likely to invest than a venture capitalist, while suppliers, joint venture partners, and institutional investors are more likely to invest in a business that's up and running and wants to expand. See Chapter 2.

Q4: Does the stage when you invest in a business project make a difference to return upon exit?

A: The earlier the investment, the greater the rewards when you exit, but you are also taking a much greater risk with your money. See Chapter 2.

Q5: How did leveraged buy-out firms give exit strategy such a poor name in the 1980s?

A: It was their "buy-and-bust" strategy. They would buy companies, break them to pieces, and sell them off. See Chapter 3.

Q6: What major role did exit strategies play in the dotcom rise and fall?

A: Spurred on by the desire not to miss out on the IPO boom, investors forgot about such basic questions as: Is this a sound business proposition? Is the management team any good? and What is the market potential? See Chapter 3, especially the timeline, and Chapter 4.

Q7: Why does private equity investing underperform in emerging markets?

A: Exits were slow to happen. There was bad timing and the US venture capital model was replicated without considering the local market. See Chapter 5.

Q8: Is driving to an IPO a good thing when trade sales are the most common form of exit?

A: Yes, you acquire a solid management team, international accounting standards and you'll have a more attractive company if you do decide to sell instead. See Chapter 6.

Q9: Why, despite the fact that there will always be circumstances beyond your control like an economic downturn, should you always have an exit strategy?

A: For investors it is the plan for realizing their return. For businesses, while an exit strategy isn't a cure-all for all aspects of business performance, it will focus decision making to the benefit of the day-to-day running of a company. Just remember a strategy isn't set in stone: you can always change it. See Chapter 6, and the Delifrance case study in Chapter 7.

Q10: Why is exit strategy the last thing that entrepreneurs think about?

A: Entrepreneurs are too busy trying to establish and run their business to give a lot of thought to the distant future. Family-run businesses are an excellent case in point – it is always assumed that the next generation will take over though it doesn't necessarily work out that way. See Chapter 6.

Index